D1672754

SvelteKit Up and Running

Leverage the power of a next-generation web framework to
build high-performance web apps with ease

Dylan Hildenbrand

BIRMINGHAM—MUMBAI

SvelteKit Up and Running

Group Product Manager: Rohit Rajkumar

Publishing Product Manager: Jane D'Souza

Senior Editor: Aamir Ahmed

Book Project Manager: Sonam Pandey

Technical Editor: Simran Ali

Copy Editor: Safis Editing

Proofreader: Safis Editing

Indexer: Hemangini Bari

Production Designer: Alishon Mendonca

DevRel Marketing Coordinator: Nivedita Pandey

First published: July 2023

Production reference: 040723

Packt Publishing Ltd

Grosvenor House

11 St Paul's Square

Birmingham

B3 1R

ISBN 978-1-80461-548-5

www.packtpub.com

To my best friend and wife, Alec, whose love and support made this book possible. You inspire me to be the best person I can be.

– Dylan Hildenbrand

Contributors

About the author

Dylan Hildenbrand is a freelance web developer and open source software enthusiast who enjoys a good challenge. The past decade of experience as a full stack developer has provided him with a broad set of skills ranging all the way from system administration to frontend development. While he enjoys working with JavaScript and Node.js, he also has years of training with PHP, WordPress, and Yii2. In his spare time, he manages his homelab, which is automated using Ansible. To read more of his ramblings about web development and why Vim is the best text editor, visit `https://www.closingtags.com`.

I want to thank my wife, Alec, for her unwavering support over the years. I want to thank my children, Nolan and Aubrey, whose curiosity invigorates me. I also want to thank my mother, Patty, who stands as an example that inspires me to read, write, and teach others.

About the reviewer

Jimmy Hogoboom is a software engineer with over a decade of experience building and maintaining secure web applications and, in darker times, Windows Forms applications.

In his previous experience, he has designed and implemented several complex enterprise data management systems and was responsible for modernizing several ancient financial transaction processing systems (Windows Forms), which eventually pushed him into learning the big, new component-based JavaScript library at the time, which shall not be named. Since then, he has produced and deployed web applications with several different JavaScript frameworks and libraries on clients, servers, and the cloud.

Table of Contents

Preface   xiii

Part 1 – Getting Started with SvelteKit

1

Initial Setup and Project Structure   3

Technical requirements	4	tests/	6
Prerequisites	4	src/	7
Installing SvelteKit	5	Hello World Application	8
SvelteKit's Project Structure	6	Summary	9
static/	6	Resources	10

2

Configurations and Options   11

Technical requirements	11	server	17
Configuring SvelteKit	12	build	17
alias	13	preview	18
appDir	14	optimizeDeps	18
csp	14	ssr	18
csrf	15	Summary	18
env	15	Further Reading	18
prerender	16		
Configuring Vite	16		
plugins	17		

3

Compatibility with Existing Standards   19

Technical requirements	20	URL	25
Fetch	20	Summary	27
FormData	23	Resources	27

Part 2 – Core Concepts

4

Effective Routing Techniques   31

Technical requirements	31	Actions	38
Creating Dynamic Pages	32	API Endpoints	40
Creating Server Pages	37	Creating Layouts	42
load()	37	Summary	44
Page options	37	Resources	44

5

Deep Dive into Data Loading   45

Technical requirements	45	Destructuring RequestEvent	52
Loading in Clients	46	Summary	56
Loading in Layouts	47	Resources	56

6

Forms and Data Submission   57

Technical requirements	57	Database setup	61
Form Setup	58	Passwords and Security	62
Analyzing Actions	60	Login Action	63

Enhancing Forms	**66**	**Summary**	**68**
enhance	66	**Resources**	**69**
Snapshots	67		

7

Advanced Routing Techniques   71

Technical requirements	72	Sorting	78
Using optional parameters	72	Encoding	78
Rest parameters	74	**Advanced layouts**	**79**
Matching, sorting, and encoding –		**Summary**	**82**
oh, my!	76	**Resources**	**82**
Matching	77		

Part 3 – Supplemental Concepts

8

Builds and Adapters   85

Technical requirements	86	adapter-cloudflare	90
Creating a Build	86	adapter-static	93
Adapting the app	88	**Summary**	**95**
adapter-node	88	**Resources**	**95**

9

Hooks and Error Handling   97

Technical requirements	97	Error Handling	106
Using Hooks	98	**Summary**	**108**
Server hooks	98	**Resources**	**109**
Shared hooks	104		

10

Managing Static Assets   111

Technical requirements	111	File Paths	116
Importing Assets	112	SvelteKit Configuration Options	116
Additional Information	115	Vite Configuration Options	116
Images versus Styles	115	**Summary**	**117**
Customizing Imports	115	**Resources**	**117**

11

Modules and Secrets   119

Technical requirements	119	Keeping secrets safe	122
SvelteKit Module Summaries	119	$env/static/private	122
$app/environment	120	$env/static/public	123
$app/forms	120	$env/dynamic/private	123
$app/navigation	120	$env/dynamic/public	123
$app/paths	121	**Summary**	**124**
$app/stores	121	**Resources**	**124**
$service-worker	122		

12

Enhancing Accessibility and Optimizing SEO   125

Technical requirements	125	Summary	130
Compile-Time Checks	126	Resources	130
Announcing routes	127		
Accessibility enhancements	128		
SEO Tips	129		

Appendix

Examples and Support   131

Technical requirements   131

Integrations   131

More Reading and Resources   135

SvelteKit Documentation   135

SvelteKit Tutorial   135

Svelte and SvelteKit chat   135

Independent Creators   135

Svelte Society   136

SvelteKit Repository   136

Wrapping up   136

Summary   136

Resources   136

Index   137

Other Books You May Enjoy   142

Preface

Hello, and welcome to *SvelteKit Up and Running*! This book aims to be an easy-to-read guide introducing you to the core concepts of the refreshingly simple **JavaScript (JS)** framework known as SvelteKit. It was written to highlight what I felt were the core concepts of the framework. Because the JS landscape changes so frequently, this text should not be considered an authority on SvelteKit. Rather, the intention behind this book is to provide a resource that I wish was available to me when I was learning this promising new framework. As I often find myself wanting to learn high-level concepts first and then move on to finer details, so this book will too. However, before we begin, we must cover a few high-level concepts.

What is SvelteKit?

SvelteKit is an all-in-one solution to develop web applications using Svelte components. If you're familiar with React, then you've likely heard of **Create React App**. While both Svelte and React are useful to create reusable components built with JS, each is more useful when given a means of utilizing those components.

Out of the box, SvelteKit provides mechanisms to handle routing; **server-side rendering (SSR)** supports TypeScript and enriches the development experience with features such as **Hot Module Replacement (HMR)**, which automatically refreshes the browser when changes are detected in an application. This feature, and many others, are made possible by the tight coupling of SvelteKit with Vite.

How does Vite simplify development?

SvelteKit, and features such as HMR, wouldn't be possible without Vite, which itself wouldn't be possible without **Rollup** and **esbuild**. Vite differentiates itself from other bundling tools by providing a lightning-fast development server that leverages native **ECMAScript Module (ESM)** availability in modern web browsers. Vite accomplishes this by breaking application code into two parts – dependencies and source code.

Dependencies

Vite can provide a fast development server by pre-bundling each dependency from a project into its own ES module with esbuild. Whether those dependencies are in **CommonJS**, **Universal Module Definition** (**UMD**), or ESM formats is irrelevant to Vite, as it will convert them all to ESM on the initial application build. Doing this means the browser only has to make a single HTTP request for each dependency instead of a request for each import statement. This can greatly improve the performance of the development server, especially considering how quickly requests can add up in dependency-heavy applications.

Source code

Unlike dependencies, source code changes often during development. To keep the developers (you) of this source code happy, Vite utilizes a couple of clever approaches. Because modern browsers support native ES modules, Vite can offload the work of bundling to the browser and only needs to transform the source code into a native ES module before serving it to the browser. The appropriate source code is then only loaded by the browser when necessary – that is, if it is used on the currently displayed screen.

To avoid the inefficiency of re-bundling an entire application each time the source code changes, Vite supports HMR. Essentially, HMR is the practice of replacing only the ES module that was changed. This keeps the development server fast, whether the application consists of a single page or thousands.

So far, we've discussed Vite and its usage of esbuild, but how does **Rollup** fit in with it all? Vite utilizes Rollup during the build process – that is, instead of shipping the source code as is, our Svelte components are transformed into pure JS, which is then easily read by browsers. Rollup manages the potentially thousands of modules included in a project with features such as tree-shaking (only including parts of modules that are used), code splitting (breaking code up into chunks), and lazy loading (only loading resources when they are needed). The usage of these features leads to smaller, and therefore, better-performing web applications.

Who is this book for?

SvelteKit Up and Running is intended for web developers looking to advance their skill set by learning the next popular JS-based framework. Whether you're deciding which JS framework should be the first you learn, or you want to set yourself apart from other job applicants by adding yet another popular technology to your résumé, this book will help provide you with all of the essentials to begin your journey to becoming a SvelteKit master! A working knowledge of HTML, CSS, JS, and Svelte will be required to maximize the value of this material.

What does this book cover?

Chapter 1, Initial Setup and Project Structure, explains how to install a new SvelteKit project and set up a development environment. It also covers how SvelteKit projects are logically structured and the best practices to organize source code.

Chapter 2, Configurations and Options, covers how to customize an application via the options available within SvelteKit and Vite configurations.

Chapter 3, Compatibility with Existing Standards, goes into detail about how SvelteKit works with modern web standards such as the Fetch, FormData, and URL **Application Programming Interfaces (APIs)**.

Chapter 4, Effective Routing Techniques, discusses basic routing techniques. These techniques are essential to creating everything, from the simplest of pages and API endpoints to dynamic URLs that change with the content. It also covers how to create a cohesive user interface for applications using layouts.

Chapter 5, Deep Dive into Data Loading, explains in detail how to get data onto our pages and into components through the use of SvelteKit's load() function. It also breaks down the data available to developers within that same function.

Chapter 6, Forms and Data Submission, covers how developers can receive data from users through the use of HTML form elements. From there, it explains how actions can be used to break up logic pertaining to forms and how those forms may be enhanced to reduce the friction often experienced by users.

Chapter 7, Advanced Routing Techniques, discusses the details behind some of the lesser-used yet more powerful features of SvelteKit's routing mechanism. It covers how developers can work with optional parameters in routes, handle routes with an unknown number of parameters, as well as the precedence of routes when conflicts are encountered.

Chapter 8, Builds and Adapters, explains how developers can prepare an application for different environments. It provides examples to prepare a SvelteKit application for deployment to Cloudflare Pages, a Node.js environment, and even static hosting solutions.

Chapter 9, Hooks and Error Handling, covers the differences between server hooks and shared hooks, as well as how they can be used to manipulate data flowing into and out of an application. Along with this, it explains how developers can manage errors that are expected and what to do about those that were never anticipated.

Chapter 10, Managing Static Assets, goes into detail as to how to best manage assets such as images or global CSS files. It explains how Vite is central to this process and the best practices.

Chapter 11, Modules and Secrets, discusses a few of the modules not covered throughout the rest of the book. It gives you a general overview of some of the other tools and functionality that come bundled with SvelteKit. It also covers the modules responsible for managing secrets such as API keys or database passwords.

Chapter 12, Enhancing Accessibility and Optimizing SEO, will showcase how simple it is to make applications available to a wider audience. Not only does incorporating these practices make applications more compatible with technologies such as screen readers, but it also provides the added benefit of enhancing rankings within search engine providers.

Appendix: Examples and Support, gives you access to both official and unofficial community-maintained resources. The examples given of how to integrate other front-end technologies with SvelteKit show just how easy it is to do, especially when community projects are leveraged to speed up the development process. The resources provided in this section are invaluable for troubleshooting issues and making friends within the SvelteKit community.

To get the most out of this book

To get the most out of this book and ensure the information provided is retained, it is recommended to work alongside the material as you read it. Type the commands and code on your device, but also feel free to experiment and play with the code as you go. You will need a working knowledge of Svelte, JS, HTML, and CSS to get the most out of this book, as it focuses solely on SvelteKit.

Software/hardware covered in the book	Operating system requirements
SvelteKit 1.16.3 or higher	Windows, macOS, or Linux
JS	
HTML and CSS	

If you are using the digital version of this book, we advise you to type the code yourself or access the code from the book's GitHub repository (a link is available in the next section). Doing so will help you avoid any potential errors related to the copying and pasting of code.

Download the example code files

You can download the example code files for this book from GitHub at `https://github.com/PacktPublishing/SvelteKit-Up-and-Running`. If there's an update to the code, it will be updated in the GitHub repository.

We also have other code bundles from our rich catalog of books and videos available at `https://github.com/PacktPublishing/`. Check them out!

Download the color images

We also provide a PDF file that has color images of the screenshots and diagrams used in this book. You can download it here: `https://packt.link/1zRGE`.

Conventions used

There are a number of text conventions used throughout this book.

`Code in text`: Indicates code words in text, database table names, folder names, filenames, file extensions, pathnames, dummy URLs, user input, and Twitter handles. Here is an example: "In this new version, we still import the `bcrypt` module, but we've also added the import of `user.json`."

A block of code is set as follows:

```
import bcrypt from 'bcrypt';
export const actions = {
  login: async ({request}) => {
    const form = await request.formData();
    const hash = bcrypt.hashSync(form.get('password'), 10);
    console.log(hash);
    console.log(crypto.randomUUID());
  }
}
```

Any command-line input or output is written as follows:

```
npm install bcrypt
```

Bold: Indicates a new term, an important word, or words that you see on screen. For instance, words in menus or dialog boxes appear in **bold**. Here is an example: "In Firefox, you can find it under **Storage | Session Storage**."

> **Tips or important notes**
> Appear like this.

Get in touch

Feedback from our readers is always welcome.

General feedback: If you have questions about any aspect of this book, email us at customercare@ packtpub.com and mention the book title in the subject of your message.

Errata: Although we have taken every care to ensure the accuracy of our content, mistakes do happen. If you have found a mistake in this book, we would be grateful if you would report this to us. Please visit www.packtpub.com/support/errata and fill in the form.

Piracy: If you come across any illegal copies of our works in any form on the internet, we would be grateful if you would provide us with the location address or website name. Please contact us at copyright@packt.com with a link to the material.

If you are interested in becoming an author: If there is a topic that you have expertise in and you are interested in either writing or contributing to a book, please visit authors.packtpub.com.

Share Your Thoughts

Once you've read *SvelteKit Up and Running*, we'd love to hear your thoughts! Scan the QR code below to go straight to the Amazon review page for this book and share your feedback.

https://packt.link/r/1-804-61548-X

Your review is important to us and the tech community and will help us make sure we're delivering excellent quality content.

Download a free PDF copy of this book

Thanks for purchasing this book!

Do you like to read on the go but are unable to carry your print books everywhere?

Is your eBook purchase not compatible with the device of your choice?

Don't worry, now with every Packt book you get a DRM-free PDF version of that book at no cost.

Read anywhere, any place, on any device. Search, copy, and paste code from your favorite technical books directly into your application.

The perks don't stop there, you can get exclusive access to discounts, newsletters, and great free content in your inbox daily

Follow these simple steps to get the benefits:

1. Scan the QR code or visit the link below

https://packt.link/free-ebook/9781804615485

2. Submit your proof of purchase

3. That's it! We'll send your free PDF and other benefits to your email directly

Part 1 –
Getting Started with SvelteKit

In this part, we'll introduce you to SvelteKit with a quick installation, followed up with the standard *Hello, World!* example we've all come to love and appreciate. This will help familiarize you with the project structure. We'll then go on to explore the various configuration options available to further customize a SvelteKit application. From there, we'll look at how SvelteKit leverages existing standards to deliver a small yet powerful framework.

This part has the following chapters:

- *Chapter 1, Initial Setup and Project Structure*
- *Chapter 2, Configurations and Options*
- *Chapter 3, Compatibility with Existing Standards*

1
Initial Setup and Project Structure

I've been developing web applications for almost a decade now and the landscape has changed drastically since I began. To put that in reference, I've been building websites since JavaScript was so poorly supported by mainstream browsers that jQuery became the de facto standard for building interactive frontend experiences. But over time, we've seen more browsers willing to support ECMAScript standards and the ones that didn't have died off (good riddance, Internet Explorer). JavaScript then re-emerged as a viable language. And with the rise of Node.js, developers could finally build an entire application, both frontend and backend, in a single programming language. JavaScript had taken over the web development world and firmly cemented its foothold.

As the technologies have matured, so too have development experiences. With the arrival of SvelteKit 1.0, we developers are given an intuitive experience allowing us to couple frontend and backend logic together in a way that leaves us wondering, "How did we do this before?" Before we dive into that experience, we'll need to cover a few things.

Firstly, we'll cover the prerequisites for developing applications with SvelteKit. We'll then move on to how SvelteKit is installed and discuss how projects are typically structured. From there, we'll build a "Hello, World!" application so we can see everything in action.

To summarize, we'll discuss these topics in this chapter:

- Prerequisites
- Installing SvelteKit
- SvelteKit's Project Structure
- "Hello, World!"

After covering all of this material, you should be reasonably comfortable setting up a new SvelteKit application for your next project.

Technical requirements

The complete code for this chapter is available on GitHub at: `https://github.com/PacktPublishing/SvelteKit-Up-and-Running/tree/main/chapters/chapter01`

Prerequisites

To get the most out of this book and ensure you retain the information provided, it is recommended to work alongside the material as you read it. Type the commands and code shown into your project, but also feel free to experiment. To do this effectively, you will need a computer running Windows, macOS, or a Linux-based operating system as well as access to a terminal or command-line interface. Most modern computer hardware capable of running the latest versions of the aforementioned operating systems should be sufficient for your needs. Specifically, you'll need a system with a minimum of 1 GB of RAM and at least a 1.6 GHz processor. This should work just fine for developing with SvelteKit, though performance may vary for your operating system.

Like many other web development projects, you'll also need a web browser. The latest version of Firefox, Chrome, or Safari is recommended. You will also need to install Node.js. It is recommended to use the latest **Long-Term Support** (**LTS**) version, which, at the time of writing this book, is version 18. An alternative and often easier method of managing Node.js installation is the **Node Version Manager** (**NVM**) project. It allows users to easily install and change versions of Node.js. See the end of this chapter for resources related to both Node.js and NVM. Alongside that, you will also need a package manager. This book will utilize npm as it is available with a standard Node.js installation. It is possible to use yarn in place of npm, but it is probably easier to just use npm. If you're worried about performance, pnpm will also work.

The final tool required will be a text editor or **Integrated Development Environment** (**IDE**). The Svelte community supports many editors, but the official SvelteKit documentation recommends using **Visual Studio Code** (**VS Code**) along with the Svelte extension. While it is not required, it can certainly ease the pain of dealing with the different syntaxes found in Svelte components. To install Svelte for VS Code, launch VS Code Quick Open with *Ctrl + P*, type `ext install svelte.svelte-vscode`, and hit *Enter*.

In summary, you will need the following:

- A macOS, Windows, or Linux-based computer
- A modern web browser (Firefox, Chrome, or Safari)
- Terminal access
- Node.js 18+ LTS
- A package manager (npm comes installed with Node.js)
- A text editor/IDE (with the recommended Svelte extension)

Installing SvelteKit

To begin, open your terminal or command-line interface and navigate to a directory where you are comfortable starting a new project. From there, we'll run three simple commands. The first will create a new SvelteKit project with various prompts to initialize the application, the second will install dependencies, and the third will start our development server:

```
npm create svelte@latest
npm install
npm run dev
```

When running the first command, you'll be presented with several prompts. The first of these will ask you to install `create@svelte` to which your response should be y for yes. When prompted to select a directory to install the project in, leave the option blank to use the current directory (or specify the directory if you'd prefer to). You'll then be asked which template to use. We'll be working primarily with the option **Skeleton project** but feel free to come back and give the **SvelteKit demo app** a try in another directory at your convenience.

The next prompt pertains to **TypeScript** (**TS**) usage, for which SvelteKit has excellent support. However, to keep the focus of this book on SvelteKit itself and to appeal to developers that may not yet be familiar with TS, we will be using plain JavaScript. As such, to properly follow along with this text, you should select **No**. If you feel comfortable enough with TS, then by all means, select **Yes**. Be sure to select **Yes** for ESLint and Prettier support as they will very likely save you headaches and further improve your development experience. It is also recommended to include supported testing packages, but this book will not be covering testing strategies.

After installing the project dependencies with npm install, we run npm run dev, which starts our development server. The output from the command should look similar to that shown in *Figure 1.1*.

Figure 1.1 – Showing the output from the Vite development server

Notice how quickly Vite starts our development server. Even though this is a bare-bones application, other bundling tools would have taken multiple seconds whereas Vite was ready in under one second. As shown in the output displayed in the terminal, the site can be viewed by navigating to `http://localhost:5173/` in your browser. If you would like to access the site from a device other than your development machine, for instance, on a mobile device, then you may append `--host` to the appropriate npm script found in the `package.json` project file. Under the `scripts` entry, the new command would look like `"dev": "vite dev --host"`.

We've just covered the installation process for SvelteKit. At this point, it should be trivial for you to install your own SvelteKit-based project. We've covered how the various prompts from the `create@svelte` package allow you to customize the project to your liking. Now, let's take a look at how a typical SvelteKit project is structured.

SvelteKit's Project Structure

Once you have installed a new SvelteKit project, open the project directory in your preferred editor. Within that folder, you'll notice files that are commonly found in the root project folder of JavaScript applications such as `package.json`, `.gitignore`, and `README.md`, as well as configuration files pertaining to SvelteKit (`svelte.config.js`) and Vite (`vite.config.js`). You'll also notice three subfolders: `static/`, `tests/`, and `src/`. Let's look at them in detail in the following sections.

static/

This folder is where you may place static assets such as `robots.txt` (your guidelines for search engine site crawlers), static images such as favicons, or even a global CSS style sheet. These files should be able to be served "as is." Files located in this folder will be available to your application logic as if they existed in the root folder of your project, that is, `/robots.txt`. You can also access them by prefixing the file path with `%sveltekit.assets%`. Note that if files here are changed, you may need to manually refresh the page to see changes. In some cases, you may even need to restart your development server as Vite has strong opinions about caching. You should not attempt to access files included in this directory programmatically. Rather, the paths should be "hardcoded" wherever the assets here are included.

tests/

Logically, tests from the Playwright package (included in the various prompts we said *yes* to) are located here. To run the Playwright browser test, use the npm script `npm run test`. Unit tests from Vitest will be included alongside your source code. For example, if you included a file called `utilities.js`, unit tests for it would live alongside it as `utilities.test.js`. Vitest is a package from the developers of Vite that enables simple testing for Vite-based applications. **Test-Driven Development (TDD)** is an excellent practice to follow to ensure code performs as it is expected to. However, it is beyond the scope of this book.

src/

You will be spending most of your time working in this folder as this is where the core logic for a SvelteKit application lives. There are a few files and directories that should be taken note of at this time:

- `routes/`
- `lib/`
- `app.html`

routes/

The first subfolder to take note of is `src/routes/`. This directory will contain most files necessary for managing SvelteKit's file-based routing mechanism. Its sibling folder `src/params/` will be covered later on, but for now, assume most logic related to managing the routes of your application is located here. As a brief example, if you'd like to add a static "about" page, then you would do so by creating `src/routes/about/+page.svelte` containing the appropriate markup and text.

lib/

Svelte components and various other utilities can be placed in the `src/lib/` subfolder. This folder may not be present in the skeleton project template so you'll have to add it on your own. It will be shown in the SvelteKit demo app. By placing your components here, you can easily reference them in `import` statements later on as the `$lib/` alias will be available throughout the application.

app.html

There are more files to cover that we will address later on, but for now, the final mention is `app.html`. This file serves as the base for the rest of your application to build off of. When opened, you'll notice it contains references to `%sveltekit.head%`, which SvelteKit uses for injecting various script and link tags, and `%sveltekit.body%`, which is used for injecting the markup generated for the application.

To recap, the `static/` directory contains files that don't frequently change, `tests/` contains tests from the Playwright package, and `src/` contains the source code of your project. Most Svelte components and other utilities you create can be placed at `src/lib/` so as to be easily accessed via the `$lib/` alias in `import` statements. If you'd like to add a new route to your application URL, you can do so by creating a `+page.svelte` file inside a directory with the corresponding name at `src/routes/`. And finally, your application will need a base to build off. That's where `app.html` comes in. I'm sure you're eager to finally build something, so let's do it.

Hello World Application

Now that we know a bit about what we're looking at in a freshly initialized SvelteKit project, it seems appropriate to build a "Hello, World!" application. We'll begin by opening `src/routes/+page.svelte` in our editor. At this point, it should only contain basic HTML code:

```
<h1>Welcome to SvelteKit</h1>
<p>Visit <a href="https://kit.svelte.dev">kit.svelte.dev</a> to
read the documentation</p>
```

Since this file lives directly inside the `src/routes/` directory and not a sub-directory, it is available in the browser as the URL's root route (i.e., /). If we were to create a new folder within the routes directory (i.e., `src/routes/hello/`) and place another +page.svelte file inside of that (i.e., `src/routes/hello/+page.svelte`), then we would make the /hello route available as a valid URL for our app. We'll cover more advanced routing techniques in later chapters, but for now, just know that to add a new route, you'll need to create a folder using the desired route name in the `routes` directory as well as a +page.svelte file.

Svelte Components

Readers familiar with Svelte will have noticed that the +page.svelte file extension is that of a Svelte component. That's because *it is* a Svelte component! As such, we can adjust the HTML in it, customize the look with CSS in `<style>` tags, write JS inside of `<script>` tags, and import other Svelte components. If you're unfamiliar with Svelte components, it's recommended to learn at least the basics before continuing further. Check out *Svelte 3 Up and Running* by *Allessandro Segala* or visit the official Svelte website (`https://svelte.dev`) for more information.

Let's make some changes to `src/routes/+page.svelte` to see what's happening. Change the inner text of the `<h1>` tag to read `Hello, World!`, like so:

```
<h1>Hello, World!</h1>
```

Thanks to Vite, the page in our browser is updated immediately after saving. If your setup has dual monitors available with code shown on one and your browser on the other, you'll quickly see how valuable **Hot Module Replacement** (**HMR**) can be. The change we've made is all well and good, but it isn't really a "Hello, World!" application if users can't change the text. For a true "Hello, World!" example, we need to show some text that has been provided by the user. The following code is an implementation showing just that:

```
<script>
  let name = 'World';
</script>
```

```
<form>
  <label for="name" >What is your name?</label>
  <input type="text" name="name" id="name" bind:value={name} />
</form>
<h1>Hello, {name}!</h1>
```

This simple Svelte component creates a variable named name with the default value of "World." From there, the HTML gives us a basic form binding the text input value to our variable and outputting the text inside an HTML <h1> tag. Thanks to Svelte's reactivity and the binding of the text input value to the name variable, the text provided is shown immediately, even as it is typed.

What is your name? Dylan

Hello, Dylan!

Figure 1.2 – The output from our "Hello, World!" component

Summary

In this chapter, we discussed some of the prerequisite knowledge and tools needed for getting started with SvelteKit. You likely already had a computer running a capable operating system with a browser installed. You may even have had the latest LTS version of Node.js installed with the npm package manager. We also briefly touched on getting your editor prepared by installing Svelte-specific extensions.

We continued by covering the installation process of SvelteKit. The prompts provided during the installation make setting up a new SvelteKit project simple and easily customized to a developer's liking.

After the project installation, we took a high-level look at SvelteKit's project structure. While the tests/ and static/ directories are fairly straightforward, some nuances lie within the src/ folder. For instance, keeping various Svelte components and other utilities in the src/lib/ folder can help keep a project from becoming difficult to navigate. Components located there are also easily accessed across application code via the $lib/ alias.

We also created a rudimentary "Hello, World!" application. It showcased how simple SvelteKit makes it to start building an application from scratch.

In the next chapter, we'll go over some of the various configuration options you may need to tweak in both SvelteKit and Vite to customize them to suit your needs.

Resources

- Node.js: `https://nodejs.org`
- NVM: `https://github.com/nvm-sh/nvm`
- SvelteKit: `https://kit.svelte.dev`
- VS Code: `https://code.visualstudio.com/`

2

Configurations and Options

In my opinion, there are few things more frustrating than working diligently on a project for weeks, only for a bug to manifest itself upon the project launch in the production environment because of a seemingly obscure configuration option. That is why this chapter will make efforts to teach you about the various options available to you before you dig in. I know you're ready to learn about SvelteKit already. I promise that I'm just as excited to get into "actually building stuff" as you are, but I assure you that there is value in learning these concepts early on. If you're hoping to rapidly develop a high-performance web application, then I believe it is in your best interest to learn these concepts before you start on your specific app.

To begin this chapter, we'll start by taking a look at how you can manage your project configuration with options available in your `svelte.config.js` file. We'll then take a brief look at some configurations with basic adapters so that you can get started. We'll also look at the options available to you in your `vite.config.js` file. It may seem strange to discuss Vite so much in a book about SvelteKit, but SvelteKit wouldn't be the tool it is without Vite.

In this chapter, we'll cover these topics:

- Configuring SvelteKit
- Configuring Vite

After we have discussed the configurations and how they'll affect your tools, you should feel more comfortable making appropriate changes to suit the needs of your next SvelteKit project.

Technical requirements

The complete code for this chapter is available on GitHub at: `https://github.com/PacktPublishing/SvelteKit-Up-and-Running/tree/main/chapters/chapter02`

Configuring SvelteKit

The essential configuration for a SvelteKit project lives inside the `svelte.config.js` file. Understanding the various options available to you will empower you to make the most of SvelteKit. While we cannot cover all available options in such a brief section, the aim of it is to cover options that you are likely to find useful. For more configuration options, see the *Further Reading* section at the end of this chapter for more resources.

To get started, go ahead and open the `svelte.config.js` file from the skeleton project in your editor. Note that it's quite simple at this point. Essentially, it imports the `adapter` function from the `@sveltejs/adapter-auto` package, specifies that function in the `kit` property of the `config` constant, and finally, exports the `config` object. We're also given a type annotation via **JSDoc**. The `config.kit` property is where we will add various other properties to customize our configuration. It should look similar to this:

```
import adapter from '@sveltejs/adapter-auto';
/** @type {import('@sveltejs/kit').Config} */
const config = {
    kit: {
        adapter: adapter()
    }
};
export default config;
```

The `adapter-auto` package is included by default when installing with `npm create svelte@latest`. It will automatically adapt your project during build time so that it can be effortlessly deployed to Vercel, Cloudflare Pages, Netlify, or Azure Static Web Apps. Because of this, `adapter-auto` is considered a **zero-config** adapter, meaning that you can use it for any of the aforementioned environments. However, even if you are using one of these environments, it is recommended to install the environment-specific adapter to your `devDependencies`. Doing so will allow you to customize options specific to that environment, since `adapter-auto` does not accept any options.

We'll discuss adapters at length in a later chapter; we'll cover how you can use the `adapter-static` package to generate a static site and how you can run SvelteKit applications on Node.js servers using `adapter-node`. For now, let's look at some other potential configuration options you may find yourself needing in the following sections.

alias

While it is very useful to have access to the `src/lib/` path via the `$lib/` alias, there may come a time where you want to access something outside of that. To do so, you can add the `alias` property to `config.kit`. For instance, if your project had a specific file for connecting to and managing a database, you could create an alias to make imports simpler. Alternatively, you may want to easily access an image from a commonly used folder. See the following code snippets demonstrating these concepts:

src/db.js

```
const db = {
    connection: 'DB connection successful!',
    // database logic goes here...
};
export default db;
```

svelte.config.js

```
import adapter from '@sveltejs/adapter-auto';
/** @type {import('@sveltejs/kit').Config} */
const config = {
    kit: {
        adapter: adapter(),
        alias: {
            db: '/src/db.js',
            img: '/src/images'
            }
        },
};
export default config;
```

src/routes/+page.svelte

```
<script>
    import db from 'db';
    import url from 'img/demo.png';
    let status = db.connection;
```

```
</script>
<p>{status}</p>
<img src={url}>
```

In this example, I've created a mock database object with a property called `connection`. In the `svelte.config.js` file, I've added two aliases – one for the mock database object and another that points to a folder of images. Then, in the `+page.svelte` file, an import is made from both of these aliases to illustrate how you might use aliases to import a single file, as well as make an import of one particular file from a directory.

This example fails to take into consideration any asynchronous code that would usually be required for database operations. It is also not considered best practice to make calls to a database directly from routes, but we'll come back to how to do that in a later chapter. While this example is quite rudimentary, it is intended to showcase the usefulness of being able to add your own aliases for specific files and directories.

appDir

This property defaults to the `_app` value and is used to determine where imported assets such as CSS and JS will be served from the built application.

csp

To aid in defending your application and its users from malicious **cross-site scripting** (**XSS**) attacks, you can implement **Content Security Policy** (**CSP**) response headers. How CSP works is beyond the scope of this book, so it is recommended to study it further before implementing these options in your configuration, as doing so without sufficient knowledge can lead to undesired consequences. The three properties that can be added to `config.kit.csp` are as follows:

- `mode: 'hash' | 'nonce' | 'auto'`: This specifies whether hashes or nonces should be used to enforce CSP. Using `auto` will use nonces for dynamically rendered pages and hashes for prerendered pages.

- `directives`: Directives specified here will be added to the `Content-Security-Policy` headers. See the official SvelteKit documentation for a full list of available options.

- `reportOnly`: This is used to report errors but still allows scripts to be loaded. Directives specified here will be added to the `Content-Security-Policy-Report-Only` headers. See the official SvelteKit documentation for a full list of available options.

While this can be helpful to prevent scripts from being loaded from external sources, you may have deliberately included scripts from a **Content Delivery Network** (**CDN**). If you have included external scripts, then depending on the CSP for your application, you may need to add `%sveltekit.nonce%` to the `nonce` property of the included script, like so:

```
<script src='YOUR_EXT_URL/script.js' nonce='%sveltekit.nonce%'>
```

csrf

To help protect your application from **cross-site request forgery** (**CSRF**) attacks, this option comes enabled by default. It prevents end users from making POST requests to your application from another origin. If you need to disable it, you can do so by setting `config.kit.csrf.checkOrigin` to `false`, like so:

```
const config = {
  kit: {
    adapter: adapter(),
    csrf: {
      checkOrigin: false
    }
  },
};
```

env

If you have included .env files in your project, you can further specify which ones can be public and which directory they are stored in with the following options:

- `dir`: A string value that defaults to “.” (the project `root` directory).
- `publicPrefix`: A string value that defaults to `PUBLIC_`. This prefix denotes whether environment variables located in .env files are safe to be exposed to client-side code. Those environment variables are then accessible by importing from the `$env/static/public` module throughout the rest of the application. For example, assume we're working with an .env file in the base directory of our project. Adding the `PUBLIC_EXTERNAL_API=https://api.nasa.gov/planetary/apod` value will be importable in client-side code, whereas the `INTERNAL_API=AN_INTERNAL_IP_ADDRESS` value will only be importable in server code.

prerender

It's very likely that at least some content in your application will be prerenderable – that is, it will show the exact same HTML, CSS, and JS for each and every user that visits it. A common example of this is an "About" page. Whether or not you would like for a specific page to be prerendered will be addressed in a later chapter, but to further customize prerendering, consider the following options that can be added to `config.kit.prerender`:

- `entries`: An array of strings for each route that should be prerendered. The default value is the `*` special character and will include all non-dynamic routes.

- `concurrency`: The number of pages that can be prerendered simultaneously. Because JS is single-threaded, this will only take effect if your project needs to make network requests during the prerendering process.

- `crawl`: This option defaults to `true`. It tells SvelteKit whether or not it should prerender pages found in the `entries` array.

- `handleHttpError`: This option defaults to `fail`. Other options include `ignore`, `warn`, or a `details` object specific to SvelteKit that implements `PrerenderHttpErrorHandler`. If the prerendering process fails at any point, this option determines how to manage it.

- `handleMissingId`: This is the same as `handleHttpError` except that the `details` object it accepts is implemented from `PrerenderMissingIdHandler`. Linking to a specific point on another page is done using a hash in the URL – a # character followed by the ID of an element on the destination page. If an element with the specified ID is not found on the destination page, then this option will determine how the build process should behave.

- `origin`: This defaults to `http://sveltekit-prerender`. If you want to use the application URL in the rendered content, it can be helpful to specify it here.

Hopefully, this list of options was not too overwhelming and gave some insight as to how you can customize SvelteKit to your needs. SvelteKit will continue to evolve, so it is always recommended to check the official documentation, as features may be added or removed in future releases.

Now that we've looked at a few options available for customizing SvelteKit, let's look at how we can modify the behavior of Vite. Like SvelteKit, Vite comes with opinions on how projects should be configured. These opinions are useful for a wide range of use cases, but there will always be instances where they'll need to be adjusted.

Configuring Vite

As previously mentioned, Vite is the build tool that makes SvelteKit possible, so it's just as important to know how to configure Vite as it is SvelteKit. That being said, Vite is highly configurable, and so for the sake of brevity (and your attention span), we'll keep it limited to only a high-level view of available options. This section is not intended to be an exhaustive list but rather a quick glance at the options available to you. For further reading, consult the resources located at the end of this chapter.

At its heart, SvelteKit is just a Vite plugin. Obviously, there is more to it than that, but when you open `vite.config.js` in a newly created SvelteKit project, you'll see what I mean. Similar to `svelte.config.js`, this configuration exports a `config` constant, with a couple of properties set – the SvelteKit plugin that is imported and the tests to include. If you answered "no" to tests during the `create@svelte` prompts, you may not see the `test` property. The configuration from the skeleton application is shown in the following code snippet:

```
import { sveltekit } from '@sveltejs/kit/vite';
const config = {
    plugins: [sveltekit()],
    test: {
        include: ['src/**/*.{test,spec}.{js,ts}']
    }
};
export default config;
```

plugins

It seems logical to start with the `plugins` property of our Vite configuration, as this book's entire premise is based around one plugin in particular. With Vite becoming more popular and seeing a rise in adoption, its ecosystem is expanding, and with that comes more plugins. Many of those plugins are developed by the community to solve common problems. And because Vite extends Rollup, many Rollup plugins also work with Vite out of the box, although not all. The Vite development team maintains several official Vite plugins, including one that enables legacy browser support. Many features and functionality can be added to your application via these plugins. Once you have found a plugin that satisfies your requirements and installed it, you will need to import and include it in the `config.plugins` array, just as SvelteKit was previously shown. Configurations for plugins vary, but typically, options are passed via the parameters of the imported function call. To find more plugins available for Vite, check out the Awesome Vite project at `https://github.com/vitejs/awesome-vite`.

server

Since Vite is running the development server you'll be working on with SvelteKit, you may need to make some changes to how that server operates. For instance, you may need to change the default port, proxy it through another server elsewhere, add support for HTTPS, or even disable HMR for testing with older browsers. In these instances and more, you will want to adjust `config.server` accordingly.

build

When building your application for your production environment, you'll likely need to make some adjustments. Whether you need to ensure the application has met specific browser compatibility or you'd like to customize Rollup's options, these settings can be found under `config.build`.

preview

Once you have built your application for your production environment, you should test it with Vite's preview functionality. Changing your preview server's options can be done by managing `config.preview`.

optimizeDeps

Occasionally, you may want to test multiple dependencies or versions of dependencies with your code to see how well they work for your project. To include or exclude dependencies from pre-bundling, or to further modify options used by `esbuild`, begin configuring `config.optimizeDeps`.

ssr

If you need to prevent dependencies from running in your server environment, you may need to manage the options available to you under `config.ssr`.

Summary

In this chapter, we covered many configuration options available for SvelteKit. We went over an example of how `config.kit.alias` might be useful for importing frequently accessed files. While we did not cover all options, we did briefly look at the `appDir`, `csp`, `csrf`, `env`, and `prerender` options and how they can affect our application.

We also glanced at some configuration options available in `vite.config.js`. For the most part, SvelteKit sets up a configuration that works for us according to the choices made in the installation prompt, but for further tweaks and plugins, we now know where to start looking in the official Vite documentation.

In the next chapter, we'll go over some existing web standards and how SvelteKit's design keeps them in mind. Existing standards present in web browsers are quickly becoming supported in other environments, including Node-based environments or even Deno and Cloudflare Workers. By leveraging these standards instead of building new ones on top of them, SvelteKit is accessible to more developers.

Further Reading

- **SvelteKit documentation** – The first stop on your troubleshooting journey should always be the official SvelteKit documentation: `https://kit.svelte.dev/docs`

- **Awesome Vite** – A collection of official and community-maintained resources or plugins that make development with Vite delightful: `https://github.com/vitejs/awesome-vite`

- **Vite documentation** – Need to modify your development server or build process? Check here for official recommendations: `https://vitejs.dev/config/`

3
Compatibility with Existing Standards

Some frameworks attempt to simplify your work as a developer by providing you with tools and functionality to wrap around common tasks, such as making network requests or managing data submitted by forms. While the intentions are noble, this strategy can have unintended consequences. For instance, when learning a new framework, developers have to master all of its intricacies to be effective. Reading about *yet another way to make network requests* can slow developers down, as time spent reading documentation is time spent *not building*. It can also prevent code portability. When the code written for application *A* is specific to framework *X*, then the code will need to be modified before being reused in application *B*, which was built with framework *Y*.

SvelteKit has a solution to this, and that solution is to do nothing. Well, not *nothing*, but rather than providing you with wrappers and functions that will require you to look up the documentation each time you go to use one, SvelteKit encourages the use of existing Web **Application Programming Interfaces** (**APIs**) and standards. By not reinventing the wheel, more developers can get started with SvelteKit quickly, since they won't have to learn abstractions for standards that they're already familiar with. Not only does it keep time spent reading documentation to a minimum, but it also requires less code to power a framework.

This chapter will cover some basic use cases of **Web APIs** and how they interact with SvelteKit. Specifically, we'll look at these examples of current web standards:

- Fetch
- FormData
- URL

An in-depth dive into each of these standards is beyond the scope of this chapter, but if you're looking for more information about them, resources will be provided at the end. After these examples, you should feel comfortable using your existing knowledge of various web standards with SvelteKit.

Technical requirements

The complete code for this chapter is available on GitHub at: `https://github.com/PacktPublishing/SvelteKit-Up-and-Running/tree/main/chapters/chapter03`.

Fetch

To begin, let's take a look at one of the most commonly used Web APIs, `fetch`. Assuming your development environment is on the latest LTS version of Node.js (v18+), you'll have access to `fetch` on the server without having to install an extra package such as `node-fetch`. That package was the most widely used package to deliver functionality, allowing developers to make network requests before `fetch` was incorporated into Node.js's core features. Since `fetch` is now also supported in every major browser, we can safely use it in both client- and server-side environments to make external and internal requests. Because SvelteKit can run in both a browser and server environment, it is safe to say that we have, in fact, "made fetch happen."

To illustrate how fetch can work in both the browser and server, let's take a look at an example. We'll create a new route by adding the `src/routes/fetch/+page.svelte` file to serve as our demo page. We'll also create `src/routes/fetch/+page.js` to get data from an actual `fetch` request. In this example, we'll utilize NASA's free *Astronomy Picture of the Day* API found at `https://api.nasa.gov/`. It's recommended to obtain an API key for regular use; however, the demonstration API key provided in the following examples will suffice for our purposes. This example makes a network request to the NASA API and shows the data received on our page.

Please note that the styles are by no means required and are only provided to make our example more digestible when viewed in the browser. We could add lots of styles and make this look fantastic, but that would take up more of our limited space on these pages. Plus, you're here to learn about SvelteKit, not CSS:

src/routes/fetch/+page.svelte

```
<script>
  export let data;
</script>

<h1>Astronomy Picture of the Day</h1>
<h2>{data.pic.title}</h2>
<div class='wrap'>
  <a href={data.pic.hdurl}><img src={data.pic.url}></a>
</div>
<p>{data.pic.explanation}</p>
```

```
<style>
  h1, h2 {
    text-align: center;
  }
  .wrap {
    max-width: 75%;
    margin: 0 auto;
    text-align: center;
  }
  img {
    max-width: 100%;
  }
</style>
```

In this file, we're simply setting up the markup for our data to populate. To get access to the data provided by the sibling +page.js file, we *must* include export let data;. If you're familiar with React or Vue, think of this as SvelteKit's method for passing props between components. If you're familiar with React of Vue, think of this as SvelteKit's method for passing props between components. After doing that, we can use the data provided in the object to populate the image title, a link to the high-resolution file, a link to the externally hosted image, and show an image description. And, of course, we've added some minimal styles. The real magic, and our fetch request, happens in the next snippet for +page.js, where we make the call to the external API:

src/routes/fetch/+page.js

```
const key = 'DEMO_KEY'; // your API key here

export function load() {
  const pic = fetch(`https://api.nasa.gov/planetary/apod?api_
key=${key}`)
  .then(response => {
    console.log('got response');
    return response.json();
  });
  return {pic};
}
```

In `+page.js`, we've created a constant where you can place your own API key. Then, we exported the `load` function, which is necessary to tell SvelteKit to run before rendering the sibling `+page.svelte` file. It can be `async` or not; SvelteKit doesn't care and will handle each case accordingly. We then create the constant `pic`, to which we can assign the promise returned from the `fetch` call. In the `fetch` call, we provided the URL with an API key appended to it, as the first and only argument. If your API needed to have options specified in the header, a method set, or perhaps an authentication cookie, you could do so by providing that as an object in the second argument. Remember that SvelteKit aims to be compatible with the existing web standards, so the implementations will have at least the standardized functionality. See the resources at the end of this chapter for more information on how to utilize `fetch` in these ways.

Continuing with the promise received by the `fetch` call, we run `console.log()` to demonstrate that code is being run in both the browser and server environments. If your development environment isn't yet running, you can start it with the `npm run dev` command. Remember that it will then be available in your browser at the provided URL. You can confirm this by checking your browser console output in your developer tools, as well as the output from your Vite development server in your terminal. In both cases, you should see the "*got response*" output displayed. Because our request didn't require any authentication, it was safe for us to run on the client side.

Finally, we convert the **Response** object body to JSON, and the entire promise is wrapped in an object so that it may be returned. As we've seen with universal `load` functions, they run on both the server and browser. In the case of universal load functions, they *must* return an object.

> **Loading Data**
>
> We've established that code run from `+page.js` is actually run in both the browser and server. If we wanted the code to only be run on the client, we would place that in `+page.svelte`. Similarly, if we wanted this code to be run only on the server, then we could change the filename to `+page.server.js`. This second use case would be more suitable for making an authenticated database call or accessing environment variables, such as API keys (as we did in this previous example). SvelteKit will recognize that this file is intended to run only in the server environment and will take the appropriate steps to separate that logic. Server `load` functions also work slightly differently from universal `load` functions, but we'll go into that in more depth in a later chapter.

After doing all of this, we can now navigate to `/fetch` in our browser and see the image, its title, and a description, and even click on the image to view the full high-resolution file. It's very helpful to make calls to various internal or external APIs, but our application will likely need to receive data from users at some point. In the next section, we'll cover how we can access and manipulate `FormData` objects provided in `Requests`.

FormData

When building web applications, it's common to accept data from users through the use of forms. Accessing this data can be done via the **FormData API**. To see this in action, let's look at a basic form that allows users to post a comment to our application. In this example, we'll create two files, +page. svelte and +page.server.js, under the new *comment* route. As before, the +page.svelte file contains HTML to scaffold our form and minimal styles. In order to get access to the data sent from our server, we must include the line reading export let form; in our client-side <script> code. This lets us view the status of the object returned from +page.server.js and report the status back to the user by using the templating system provided by Svelte:

src/routes/comment/+page.svelte

```
<script>
  export let form;
</script>
<div class='wrap'>
  {#if form && form.status === true}
    <p>{form.msg}</p>
  {/if}
  <form method='POST'>
    <label>
      Comment
      <input name="comment" type="text">
    </label>
    <button>Submit</button>
  </form>
</div>
<style>
  .wrap {
    width: 50%;
    margin: 0 auto;
    text-align: center;
  }
  p {
    color: green;
```

```
    }
  label {
    display: block;
    margin: 1rem;
  }
</style>
```

src/routes/comment/+page.server.js

```
export const actions = {
  default: async (event) => {
    const form = await event.request.formData();
    const comment = form.get('comment');
    if(comment) {
      // save comment to database
      return {
        status: true,
        msg: `Your comment has been received!`
      }
    }
  }
}
```

As noted earlier, +page.server.js works in the same way as a +page.js file, except that it will only run on the server. Just as we can export load(), like in our fetch example, server-side files can also export actions. These exported actions can only be accessed via POST requests. We'll look at how we can further utilize actions in a later chapter, but for now, note that we're creating a single action, default. This means that when a form is submitted, the POST request is handled by the /comment endpoint.

From the default action, this example accesses the Request object located in event, and then accesses FormData within that Request. Once the FormData object has been assigned to the form variable, we use get() to retrieve the value from the form input by its name. Normally, we would then move on to something akin to a database call that would save the comment alongside a unique user identifier. For the sake of brevity, we will just return an object with the status and msg properties.

When the page reloads, those properties are then checked by the Svelte template syntax and show the user a message that their comment has been successfully submitted. Even though this example only accessed `FormData` with `get()`, all methods documented in official standards are also available to us. If we wanted to cycle through all values and keys submitted, we could do so using a `for...of` loop and access the values via `form.values()` and `form.keys()`.

Now that we know how to obtain data from submitted forms, we should also look at another way of receiving data from users that may be overlooked – the URL.

URL

The **URL API** can be helpful in instances where you need to parse your application's URL. SvelteKit makes accessing the URL API quite simple, as it is also available in the `event` object, just as the `request` object was. Let's continue with our previous example using comments. If we wanted to build a commenting service for use across a network of other websites, we may want to report to a user which site they just commented on. Let's expand on that previous example and do just that. We don't need to make any changes to `src/routes/comment/+page.svelte`. Instead, we'll adjust our server action accordingly.

This example is identical to the last except for a couple of changes. The URL API is accessed via `event.url` and assigned to the `url` constant. It is then output to the server with `console.log(url)` to show you the various read-only properties that you can access. For this demonstration, we get the hostname via `url.hostname` and use it in a template literal, which is assigned to the `msg` property of the returned object:

src/routes/comment/+page.server.js

```
export const actions = {
  default: async (event) => {
    const form = await event.request.formData();
    const url = event.url;
    console.log(url);

    const comment = form.get('comment');
    if(comment) {
      // save comment to DB here
      return {
        status: true,
        msg: `Your comment at ${url.hostname} has been
          received!`
      }
```

```
        }
    }
}
```

If you switch to your browser window and post a comment, you'll now see that it reports the `hostname` property. In a production environment, this would ideally be your domain name, but in our development environment, we see the message **Your comment at 127.0.0.1 has been received!**. If you've accessed your development site from `http://localhost`, you'll see **localhost** instead of the IP address. Switch back to your terminal where the development server is running, and you'll see the various read-only properties that you have access to within the URL object:

Sample event.url object

```
URL {
    href: 'http://127.0.0.1:5173/comment',
    origin: 'http://127.0.0.1:5173',
    protocol: 'http:',
    username: '',
    password: '',
    host: '127.0.0.1:5173',
    hostname: '127.0.0.1',
    port: '5173',
    pathname: '/comment',
    search: '',
    searchParams: URLSearchParams {},\
    hash: ''
}
```

This URL object showcases how simple it is to grab information about it. All of the read-only properties shown are easily accessed using dot notation. Gone are the days of parsing an entire URL with regex in an attempt to extract the portion needed. Now, if you wanted to get the values set in query strings, you could easily iterate over `event.url.searchParams` with a `for...of` loop. Go ahead and add some options to the URL in your browser. An example might look like `http://127.0.0.1:5173/comment?id=5&name=YOUR_NAME_HERE`. Now, the `console.log(url)` function call will output the names and values set after the first ? and each subsequent &.

Summary

In this chapter, we covered an example use case of `fetch` and a two-part demonstration showing how `URL` and `FormData` can be used. While the examples presented here do not represent the full scope of the various Web APIs that you'll have access to, they should illustrate how simple it is to use them with SvelteKit. If you're hoping to build applications with SvelteKit, it's important you become familiar with these modern Web APIs, as they're used extensively throughout development with SvelteKit. SvelteKit encourages you to lean on that existing knowledge. By doing so, SvelteKit can ship less code to you so that you can ship less code to your users.

In the next chapter, we'll move away from the background information that is necessary for using SvelteKit and start building something that resembles an application. We'll cover various routing techniques and how you can build out a consistent user interface across the application.

Resources

- MDN Web Docs – For references to `fetch()`, `formData()`, `URL`, and more, visit `https://developer.mozilla.org`.

Part 2 – Core Concepts

Navigation on the web is such a quintessential experience that the developers of SvelteKit have made routing central to the framework. In this part, we'll examine previously introduced routing techniques in more detail. After that, we'll see how SvelteKit moves data to components and accepts data from them through HTML form elements. Finally, we'll see some more advanced routing techniques that promise to cover even the most obscure edge cases encountered in routing.

This part has the following chapters:

- *Chapter 4, Effective Routing Techniques*
- *Chapter 5, Deep Dive into Data Loading*
- *Chapter 6, Forms and Data Submission*
- *Chapter 7, Advanced Routing Techniques*

4

Effective Routing Techniques

We've spent a lot of time covering background information. I know those topics aren't always the most exciting, but now that we've covered them, we can get to the real fun. Up until now, we've only briefly touched on adding new routes by creating a directory inside `src/routes/` with the desired route name and adding a `+page.svelte` file inside of it. We also briefly looked into creating server pages. But, of course, routing isn't always so simple. How do we build out an **application programming interface (API)**? How do we create a consistent **user interface (UI)** throughout our application without duplicating styles on each page? What happens when our application throws an error?

In this chapter, we will answer some of those questions by discussing some core points about routing within the context of SvelteKit. First, we'll look at how we can create new pages with dynamic content. Then, we'll take a closer look at how the `+page.server.js` files work. We'll then show how to go about creating API endpoints that can accept various types of HTTP requests. And finally, we'll cover how to build a consistent UI throughout an application using layouts.

In this chapter, we'll cover the following topics:

- Creating Dynamic Pages
- Creating Server Pages
- Creating API Endpoints
- Creating Layouts

By the end of this chapter, you should have a comfortable understanding of routing concepts for SvelteKit's file-based routing mechanism.

Technical requirements

The complete code for this chapter is available on GitHub at: `https://github.com/PacktPublishing/SvelteKit-Up-and-Running/tree/main/chapters/chapter04`.

Creating Dynamic Pages

In previous chapters, we've covered the process of creating a new page. To refresh your memory, it is as simple as creating a new directory inside `src/routes/` with the desired route name. Inside that directory, we create `+page.svelte`, which is simply a Svelte component that is then rendered as the page shown in the browser. An embarrassingly simple **About** page might look like this:

src/routes/about/+page.svelte

```
<div class='wrapper'>
  <h1>About</h1>
  <p>
    Lorem ipsum dolor sit amet...
  </p>
</div>
```

This example illustrates just how simple adding a new page is. In it, we see a `div`, an `h1` title tag, and a paragraph p tag with the `lorem ipsum` sample text. Of course, in a real-world scenario, it would have much more content as well as some styles. This example exists only to show how simple it is to add a new, static page.

But what if you needed to create a page where you didn't know what the content was? What if we wanted to create a page with a dynamic URL? For instance, when viewing news articles online, users can typically share a link directly to the article. This means each article has its own unique URL. If we wanted to create a single template that showed articles pulled from a database, we would need to find a way to manage the URL to each as well.

In instances such as these, SvelteKit's file-based routing mechanism has a special syntax to use. When creating the template showing the content, we create it in a directory with the dynamic portion of the route surrounded by square brackets ([ ]). The name given inside the brackets will then become a parameter that will allow us to load data dynamically. To make this parameter optional, use double square brackets ([[ ]]).

That may sound confusing at first, so let's take a look at an example showcasing how you might manage news articles or blog posts. We'll need to create a few files within this example. Instead of connecting to an actual database, we'll use a JSON file to store some sample data and pull directly from that:

src/lib/articles.json

```
{
  "0": {
    "title": "First Post",
    "slug": "first-post",
    "content": "Lorem ipsum dolor..."
```

```
  },
  "1": {
    "title": "Effective Routing Techniques",
    "slug": "effective-routing-techniques",
    "content": "Lorem ipsum dolor…"
  }
}
```

This file is essentially a single object containing two objects, each of which has the `title`, `slug`, and `content` properties. You can tweak this file however you like or add as many entries as you'd like to see. Its purpose is to act as a placeholder database to illustrate the following example.

Next, a news page usually has a landing page where users can scroll and view the most recent articles. In accordance with established practices, we'll create a `+page.server.js` file to load our data and make it available to the `+page.svelte` template that will function as the page rendering the data:

src/routes/news/+page.server.js

```javascript
import json from '$lib/articles.json';
export function load() {
  return { json };
}
```

Because it doesn't contain any environment variables or secrets or make a call to a real database, this file could just as well be a `+page.js` file. It works only to load data from the JSON example file. Essentially, it imports that file and then returns it as an object in the exported `load()` function, making it available to the Svelte template shown next. In reality, something so trivial could also be done in the `<script>` tag of the Svelte template but remember that this example aims to function as a stand-in for a real database.

Now that we've loaded our articles, we'll need somewhere to show them, so let's do that now and create a landing page for our news. For the sake of brevity, styles have been omitted:

src/routes/news/+page.svelte

```svelte
<script>
  export let data;
</script>
<h1>
  News
</h1>
<ul>
  {#each Object.entries(data.json) as [key, value]}
    <li>
```

```
      <a href='/news/{value.slug}'>{value.title}</a>
    </li>
  {/each}
</ul>
```

This Svelte component exports the data variable, giving us access to the data we previously returned from our faked database in load(). It then adds an h1 title tag, followed by an unordered list of each of the entries from our fake data. After which, it makes use of the {#each} Svelte template syntax to iterate over each of the entries in the array returned from Object.entries(data.json). For each of the entries (our two sample objects), we surround them with list item tags and show the title property inside a <a> tag linking to the article via the slug property.

Next, we'll need to create a page to show the article content but keep in mind we want the route to have a parameter within it, so we'll use the [ ] square brackets to surround the article slug:

src/routes/news/[slug]/+page.svelte

```
<script>
  export let data;
</script>
<h1>News</h1>
<h2>{data.title}</h2>
<div class='content'>
  {data.content}
</div>
<a href='/news'>Back to news</a>
```

This file exports the data variable so that we may access information about our article. It then shows News inside a <h1> title tag, followed by a <h2> title tag with the article title, a div containing the article content, and a link back to the news page. All of the article information is loaded by making another call to our *database* in the next file:

src/routes/news/[slug]/+page.server.js

```
import json from '$lib/articles.json';
import { error } from '@sveltejs/kit';
export function load({ params }) {
  let found = {};
  Object.keys(json).forEach((id) => {
    if(json[id].slug === params.slug) {
      found = json[id];
    }
  });
  if(Object.keys(found).length !== 0) {
```

```
    return found;
  }
  throw error(404, 'Whoops! That article wasn\'t found!');
}
```

Just as before, we've imported our fake database to access the full article content. This code also imports the `error` module from SvelteKit, which will come in handy later on. We've then exported the `load()` function so that we can return the loaded data to the rendered page. Inside the `load()` function, the code initializes an empty variable labeled `found`, and then begins to iterate over each object inside of the JSON data. In the loop, it checks whether any of the slugs in our data match the given slug in the URL. If a match is found, it is then assigned to the `found` variable. After finishing the loop, we check that `found` is not an empty object. If it is not empty, we return an object containing the `found` variable. If it is empty, we throw a **404 Not Found** error.

Upon opening your development site in your browser and navigating to /news, you should see two article titles listed. When clicked, they will redirect users to the respective article. This example illustrates routing with parameters in a simple way that works for the most part. But what do we do about the times when it doesn't work? Have you tried navigating to an article that doesn't exist yet? Go ahead and try it now; I'll wait right here:

404

Whoops! That article wasn't found!

Figure 4.1 – A generic error page is shown when throwing an error in SvelteKit

The article doesn't exist, and the user is shown a generic error page. If we didn't throw an error at all, the page would be rendered showing the `undefined` values. Instead, we should show the user a proper error page. Just as SvelteKit provides us with the +page.svelte, +page.js, and +page.server.js files, we can also create an +error.svelte template, which can be used when errors are thrown from the application. By specifying it in the src/routes/news/[slug]/ directory, the error page template will be localized to that particular route. If we wanted to build a generic error page to be used across the entire application, we could do so by placing an +error.svelte template at the root route of the application (src/routes/+error.svelte). Let's create a template in src/routes/news/[slug]/ so users aren't confused by our lack of clear communication:

src/routes/news/[slug]/+error.svelte

```
<script>
  import { page } from '$app/stores';
</script>
<h1>News</h1>
<h2>{$page.status}</h2>
```

```
<div class='content'>
  {$page.error.message}
</div>
<style>
  * {
    font-family: sans-serif;
  }
  h1, h2, .content {
    text-align: center;
    color: #358eaa;
  }
</style>
```

For this error template, we import the `page` store module to access information about this particular request. This module, as well as many others, is available to use throughout the application. As this one makes use of Svelte's stores, we can access the values it contains about the page by prefacing it with a dollar sign (`$`). The rest of this template is fairly straightforward. It includes the `<h1>` title tag labeled `News`, followed by the status code and error message we passed when we threw our error in `+page.server.js`. Some styles have been included to show how this template is different from the default template shown throughout SvelteKit. Compare *Figure 4.1* of the generic SvelteKit error template to *Figure 4.2*, our custom version:

News

404

Whoops! That article wasn't found!

Figure 4.2 – A customized error page template

By now, you should feel comfortable creating essential routes for your application, whether they are static or dynamic. You should also be able to show error pages based on the route. There will be more about advanced routing later on, but for now, let's take a closer look at how the `+page.server.js` files work.

Creating Server Pages

In previous examples, we've used the +page.js and +page.server.js files for loading data. Often, they can be used interchangeably, but when is the best time to use which? In this section, we'll break down some of the differences between the two and also discuss various features available in the +page.server.js files. We'll break it down into these topics:

- load()
- Page options
- Actions

load()

As we've seen in previous examples, data can be loaded into a +page.svelte component by exporting the data property on that page. Both +page.js and +page.server.js can then be used for loading data to that page template as they can both export a load() function. When to use which file depends on how you plan to load that data. When run in a +page.js file, load() will run on *both the client and the server*. It is recommended to load data here if you are able, as SvelteKit can manage grabbing data from calls with fetch(). This becomes particularly useful when preloading data (anticipating what the user may do and starting the process milliseconds before they actually do it).

However, there are times this isn't possible. For instance, if you need to make a call to an API that requires authentication or a database, you likely don't want your connection secrets exposed to the client. That would allow anyone with access to your application to then download your secrets and make requests to said API or database on your behalf. In these cases, you'll need to store the secrets on your server. And since those secrets are on your server, you'll need access to the server's filesystem. The server will need to make the calls to obtain the appropriate data and pass that data to the client. In instances such as these, it is best to use the +page.server.js files for data loading requirements.

Page options

+page.js and +page.server.js files are not just used for loading data. They can also export various options specific to their sibling page. Some options allow you to configure functionality related to the rendering of pages. These particular options are Boolean values, which means they can be enabled by setting them to true or disabled by setting them to false. They are the following:

- prerender
- ssr
- csr

prerender

While prerendering can be customized in a `svelte.config.js` project, you may find yourself needing to explicitly enable or disable it on a per-page basis. To enable it on a page, you can set `export const prerender = true;`. Conversely, setting its value to `false` will disable prerendering for that page. When to prerender a page should be determined by whether or not the HTML content of the page is static. If the HTML shown on the page should be the same no matter who is viewing it, then a page is considered safe to prerender. By prerendering a page, the HTML will be generated at build time, and static HTML will be shipped to the client for each request to that particular route. This results in faster load times for end users, which makes for a better experience.

Server-side rendering

Server-side rendering (**SSR**) can be a powerful tool in your arsenal to speed up the user experience. Instead of forcing the client to load a library that manages all of the rendering of content, the server will take over that responsibility so that it may ship static HTML to the client, which will then hydrate the page with data. To enable SSR for a particular route, set `export const ssr = true;` in the `+page.js` file or `+page.server.js`. SvelteKit enables this option by default, so if you need to change it, you'll likely find yourself disabling it by setting the value to `false`.

Client Side Rendering

Instead of rendering the page on the server, and sending that to the client, enabling **client-side rendering** (**CSR**) will force the client to handle the workload of rendering. This can be useful when creating a **single-page application** (**SPA**), as routing will then be managed on the client device. Be warned that if you have disabled both SSR and CSR, nothing on the page will be rendered. Instead, you'll see an empty shell of a page. To disable CSR, set `export const csr = false;` just as you would with other available page options.

You'll likely find these rendering-related options useful should you find yourself building an SPA, a static HTML site, or if you're attempting to render static content on the client end.

Actions

Because `+page.js` files are also run in the client, they cannot export actions. Actions allow you to receive data submitted by the `form` elements sent via the POST HTTP method. We saw an example of this in *Chapter 3*, where we discussed the `FormData` API compatibility with SvelteKit. In that example, we exported a default action. A default action will be triggered by submitting a form element that has not specified an `action` property. However, we are not limited to only default actions, as SvelteKit also enables us to create named actions. Named actions will all work on the same route but are differentiated from each other by providing the route followed by the action name in a query string. A default action may not exist alongside named actions, so you must remove it or change its name and set the `action` property on the `form` elements that utilize it.

Building from our previous example, let's look at how we might implement a few more actions related to comments online. Some additional functionality we may want to create would be allowing users to star a comment or reply. Since we'll be adding more named actions, we'll change the default action to create:

src/routes/comment/+page.server.js

```
export const actions = {
  create: async (event) => {
    const form = await event.request.formData();
    ...
  },
  star: async () => {
    return {
      status: true,
      msg: 'You starred this comment!'
    }
  },
  reply: async () => {
    return {
      status: true,
      msg: 'You replied!'
    }
  }
}
```

Notice how the default action was changed to create. The code within create has been omitted as it has not changed since our last example. We've also added the star and reply actions. For now, they don't do much except return an object that will output our message, showcasing that they are both called when the respective button is clicked. In a real-world scenario, these would likely make calls to a database, increasing the "star count," or saving the reply comment content and a unique identifier of the comment being replied to.

As for the form itself, we could create separate forms and specify the POST method as well as the action property for each new feature. However, a more intuitive user experience would consolidate the features and keep them all in one cohesive component. Instead of creating multiple forms, we'll create a button for the new features and specify a formaction property for each. Doing this will keep the HTTP method specified in the parent form but allow sending the requests to different actions based on the button clicked:

src/routes/comment/+page.svelte

```
<script>
  import { enhance } from '$app/forms';
  export let form;
```

```
</script>
<div class='wrap'>
  {#if form && form.status === true}
    <p>{form.msg}</p>
  {/if}
  <form method='POST' action='?/create' use:enhance>
    <label>
      Comment
      <input name="comment" type="text">
    </label>
    <button>Submit</button>
    <button formaction='?/star'>Star</button>
    <button formaction='?/reply'>Reply</button>
  </form>
</div>
<style>
...
</style>
```

The first change to notice from our previous encounter with this example is that we've added `import { enhance } from '$app/forms';`. This addition will allow us to progressively enhance our form with JavaScript. The page will then not need to be reloaded after each form submission. This module is utilized in the `<form>` element further down with the Svelte `use:` directive. Try running the example without it and observe how the URL will now contain query strings based on which button is clicked.

Speaking of buttons, we've added two in this example. Each has the `formaction` property set, which allows us to specify which of our named actions we would like called from `+page.server.js`. Take note that we *must* call these actions by specifying a query parameter followed by a / character. We've also set the form action to `?/create`. Since we have exported named actions, we can no longer have an action named `default` and must specify the action to be called on the `form` element. If we wanted to call an action located at another route, we could do so easily by setting `formaction` to the desired route name followed by `?/`, and the action name.

You should now be confident in knowing when to use `+page.server.js` over `+page.js`, how to customize the rendering of pages, and how you can easily accept data from the `form` elements. In the next section, we'll cover how you can create API endpoints that accept more than just POST requests.

API Endpoints

We've covered the `+page.svelte`, `+page.js`, and `+page.server.js` files but we have yet to discuss `+server.js` files. These files enable us to accept more than just POST requests. As web application developers, we may be expected to support various platforms. Having an API simplifies the transmission of data between our server and these other platforms. Many APIs can accept GET and POST requests as well as PUT, PATCH, DELETE, or OPTIONS.

A +server.js file creates an API endpoint by exporting a function with the name of the HTTP request method you would like for it to accept. The functions exported will take a SvelteKit-specific RequestEvent parameter and return a Response object. As an example, we can create a simple endpoint that would allow us to create posts for a blog. This could be useful if we used a mobile app to write and post from. Note that a +server.js file should not exist alongside page files as it is intended to handle all HTTP request types:

src/routes/api/post/+server.js

```js
import { json } from '@sveltejs/kit';
export function POST({ request }) {
  // save post to DB
  console.log(request);
  return json({
    status: true,
    method: request.method
  });
}
export function GET({ request }) {
  // retrieve post from DB
  console.log(request);
  return json({
    status: true,
    method: request.method
  });
}
```

This file imports the json module from the @sveltejs/kit package, which is useful for sending JSON-formatted Response objects. We then export functions named for both POST and GET methods, each of which only outputs the Request object to the console and then returns a Response JSON. If we were so inclined, we could also export functions for other HTTP verbs such as PUT, PATCH, or DELETE.

You should demo this example by navigating to the api/post/ route in your browser. After opening the page, observe the rest of the properties available in the Request object output to your development server. If you don't understand what you're looking at, that's okay because we'll look into it more in the next chapter. Back in your browser, open the **Network** tab in your developer tools, select the GET request, right-click it, select **Edit and Resend**, and change the request method to POST. Once done, send it and view the output. You should see the object with the method property set to POST returned in a JSON formatted object. If your browser doesn't allow you to edit requests, proxy tools such as OWASP ZAP, Burp Suite, Postman, or Telerik Fiddler will let you customize HTTP requests. See the resources at the end of this chapter for links.

Now that you know how to go about creating your very own API, let's look at how you can unify the user experience of your application with a layout.

Creating Layouts

We've covered a lot so far in this chapter, but we've still only added styles and markup to each specific page. This is repetitive and not a practical use of our time. To reduce repetition, we can utilize layouts. A +layout.svelte component can unify the user experience by leveraging Svelte's <slot> directive. The layout file will nest any sibling page components and child routes within itself, allowing us to show persistent markup across the application. Just like +page.svelte, we can include a +layout.svelte component at any level in our route hierarchy, allowing the nesting of layouts within layouts. Because each layout is also a Svelte component, the styles will be localized to that particular component and will not cascade to those nested within. Let's look at how we might use layouts to create a consistent layout and navigation menu for our existing code:

src/routes/+layout.svelte

```
<script>
  import Nav from '$lib/Nav.svelte';
</script>
<div class='wrapper'>
  <div class='nav'>
    <Nav />
  </div>
  <div class='content'>
    <slot />
  </div>
  <div class='footer'>
    This is my footer
  </div>
</div>
<style>
  .wrapper {
    min-height: 100vh;
    display: grid;
    grid-template-rows: auto 1fr auto;
  }
  .footer {
    text-align: center;
    margin: 20px 0;
  }
</style>
```

Because this +layout.svelte component is at the root level of our routes, it will be applied across all child routes. The very first thing our component does is import our custom navigation component (shown next). Secondly, it creates the markup that will house the rest of our application, including this file's sibling +page.svelte. Its markup consists of several <div> elements with varying class names indicating functionality. The .wrapper <div> element wraps all others so that we may apply the sticky footer styles found in the <style> section of this component. The div with the .nav class contains our custom Nav component, the .content div contains our Svelte <slot> directive, and .footer is where we would put our site footer information. Now let's take a look at the custom Nav component we imported in our root layout:

src/lib/Nav.svelte

```
<nav>
  <ul>
    <li><a href='/'>Home</a></li>
    <li><a href='/news'>News</a></li>
    <li><a href='/fetch'>Fetch</a></li>
    <li><a href='/comment'>Comment</a></li>
    <li><a href='/about'>About</a></li>
    <li><a href='/api/post'>API</a></li>
  </ul>
</nav>
<style>
  ul {
    list-style: none;
    text-align: center;
  }
  ul li {
    display: inline-block;
    padding: 0;
    margin: 1em .75em;
  }
</style>
```

This component merely contains HTML with links to all of the routes we've already created and some rudimentary styling. It consists of the <a> elements with the href properties set to the relative routes we've created up to this point. They are all nested within list items of an unordered list, contained within a <nav> element. Again, this example is overly simple, but for our purposes, it works. Now, you can add any new routes we create later on in the book to the navigation menu so they may be easily accessed when testing in the browser.

> **Relative routes**
>
> Notice how the routes provided are relative and are not prefaced by a domain name. If we were to deploy our production application to a subdirectory; rather than the root folder of our domain, these routes would fail. Instead, we can set the base path of our application in `svelte.config.js`. Specifically, we'd set `config.kit.paths.base` to our subdirectory path, starting with a `/`. Then in components and routes, we could use `import { base } from $app/paths` and preface all routes with `{base}/`. In this way, our application would know it exists within a subdirectory. Try doing it in your development project and observe how Vite and SvelteKit automatically serve the project from that directory!

To practice the concepts surrounding layouts further, try creating `src/routes/news/[slug]/+layout.svelte` to give the articles a consistent appearance. Just as we saw with the `+page.svelte` files, the `+layout.svelte` files can be accompanied by the `+layout.js` or `+layout.server.js` files. Their functionality is identical to their page counterparts, but the data returned from them will be available in `+layout.svelte` as well as any `+page.svelte` pages that exist in parallel. Page options can also be set in layout files, and those options will "trickle down" to nested components.

With the information provided, you should now have the skills necessary to produce consistent and robust UIs for your SvelteKit applications. Layouts come in handy when creating all sorts of UI elements, but especially those that must remain consistent across various portions of the app.

Summary

In this chapter, we covered how to create static and dynamic routes as well as manage custom error templates for those routes. We also saw how developers can accept data submitted via the `<form>` elements with multiple named actions that can be called from a single form. We learned how to leverage SvelteKit's routing mechanism to build out an API, which is particularly useful when an application needs to be accessed from platforms other than web browsers. We then unified the UI of our application with layouts. With those layouts, we saw how they can be leveraged to keep navigation elements in a predictable location across the app. That's a lot of information to absorb in these few pages so we'll take a closer look at some of these concepts in the next few chapters.

In the next chapter, we will learn more about managing the data we're loading onto our pages. We'll also cover more advanced methods for loading that data.

Resources

HTTP Proxy/Sending Tools:

- OWASP ZAP (Web App Penetration Testing and Proxy): `https://www.zaproxy.org/`.

- Burp Suite (Web App Penetration Testing and Proxy): `https://portswigger.net/burp`.

- Postman (API Testing Tool): `https://www.postman.com/`

- Telerik Fiddler (Web Debugging and Proxy Tool): `https://www.telerik.com/fiddler`.

5

Deep Dive into Data Loading

Every application ever created has been driven by data. Without data to process, an application is effectively useless. That's why it's very important for developers to have a firm understanding of how to manage the retrieval of that data for their application. When working with SvelteKit, this is done by exporting a load() function in page or layout files.

In the previous chapter, we briefly touched on load(). In this chapter, we'll analyze it further by discussing how it works and by looking at more practical, real-world examples of making use of it. We'll create an example of forcing load() in the client only as well as covering some key details to remember when using load(). We'll also use load() in layouts to showcase how it can make data portable across our application. Finally, we'll look at an example of making use of some of the data provided in a server load() function that is unavailable in universal load() functions.

We're going to cover the following topics in this chapter:

- Loading in Clients
- Loading in Layouts
- Destructuring RequestEvent

By the time you've finished this chapter, you'll be comfortable with all the various ways you can load data in your SvelteKit application.

Technical requirements

The complete code for this chapter is available on GitHub at: `https://github.com/PacktPublishing/SvelteKit-Up-and-Running/tree/main/chapters/chapter05`.

Loading in Clients

While discussing *Creating Server Pages* in the previous chapter, we covered how a `load()` function exported from +page.js will run on both the client and the server. When we want to ensure load is only run on the server, we move it to +page.server.js. But what if you're trying to build an offline-ready application? You may be building a **Progressive Web App (PWA)**, a **Single-Page App (SPA)**, or both! For the sake of demonstration, let's assume you want as much logic as possible to be managed on the client rather than your server. In this case, you'll want `load()` functions to run on the client and not on the server. How can we do that when a `load()` function from +page.js runs in both environments?

Again, think back to the *Creating Server Pages* section in the previous chapter where we discussed page options, and you'll remember the `ssr` option. When exported, this constant will disable or enable **Server-Side Rendering** based on the Boolean value we've provided it. To make a `load()` function in +page.js run only in the client, we can add `export const ssr = false;`. Let's go back to our `fetch` example from *Chapter 3* and modify it to demonstrate this.

Before making this adjustment, ensure the `console.log('got response')` function still exists. Open the `/fetch` route in your browser and confirm the output is shown in both the browser console and your development server. Once you've done so, disable SSR on the page by exporting the `ssr` page option:

src/routes/fetch/+page.js

```
const key = 'DEMO_KEY'; // your API key here
export const ssr = false;
export function load() {
  const pic = fetch(`https://api.nasa.gov/planetary/apod?api_
key=${key}`)
    .then(response => {
      console.log('got response');
      return response.json();
    });
  return {pic};
}
```

This example is identical to when we saw it earlier, except that on line 3, we've added `export const ssr = false;`. This page option effectively disables SSR for the page, meaning that `load()` is only ever run in the client. You'll notice the `console.log()` call isn't output to the development server anymore but does show in the browser console.

From here on out, we'll differentiate `load()` functions as either **universal** or **server**. Obviously, server `load()` functions are run on the server in +page.server.js, which means that universal `load()` functions are run from +page.js. At a high level, they are functionally identical. But there are a few idiosyncrasies to mention:

- Both universal and server `load()` functions can access data related to the request that called it.

- A server `load()` function will have access to more request data, such as cookies and the client IP address.

- Universal `load()` functions always return an object. The values of that object may be nearly anything.

- Server `load()` functions *must* return data that can be serialized by the `devalue` package (essentially, anything that can be converted into JSON). Find out more about `devalue` at `https://github.com/rich-harris/devalue`.

> **Universal Load Timing**
>
> It should be mentioned that on the first render, `load()` will execute on the server and client. Each subsequent request will then be executed in the client only. To demonstrate this behavior, navigate your browser to a route that has `load()` run from a +page.js file, like our /fetch example from *Chapter 3*. Observe the console output in the server as well as the client when initially opening the /fetch page in your browser. Navigating to another route and back will show the output only in the client.

One final note about calling `load()`; it will always be invoked at runtime unless you have specified that the page should be prerendered by way of page options. If you have decided to prerender the page, then `load()` will be called at build time. Remember that pages should only be prerendered if the static HTML shown should be the same for each user to access the page.

We've just covered how `load()` can be forced to run only on the client and some details about how it works. With all of this new information as well as the information from previous chapters, you should feel relatively comfortable about the fundamentals of `load()`. Let's expand on it and take a look at how it might be used in a layout template.

Loading in Layouts

So far, we've only looked at `load()` being used in +page.js or +page.server.js files, but it can also be utilized in +layout.js or +layout.server.js files. While layouts cannot export actions, they are otherwise functionally identical to page files. This means that previously mentioned page options (such as `ssr`) and `load()` functions will apply to any components nested inside of the layout. Another important quality to understand about `load()` functions is that because they are run concurrently within SvelteKit, a single page will not render until all requests have completed. Having a `load()` function on a page as well as a layout will prevent rendering until both have completed. But because they will be run simultaneously, any delays should be negligible.

When loading data in a layout, the most obvious advantage of doing so is the ability to access that data in sibling and child pages. This means that any data loaded by a layout can then be accessed within an inherited +page.svelte file when it has exported the data variable. SvelteKit will also keep track of data loaded across the application and only trigger load() when it believes it to be absolutely necessary. In instances where we want to force data to be reloaded, we can import the invalidate or invalidateAll modules provided by $app/navigation.

To demonstrate these concepts, let's create a component alongside the navigation that can alert the user to unread notifications. The component will persist across the application header so it may be easily accessed. This makes for an ideal scenario showcasing loading data from a layout. We'll also create another page that shows the full list of notifications to demonstrate how data loaded from a layout can be used in a child component.

Let's start with the load() function in +layout.js. For simplicity's sake, we'll return the data directly within the function call instead of making a call to an imaginary database or API:

src/routes/+layout.js

```js
export function load() {
  console.log('notifications loaded');
  return {
    notifications: {
      count: 3,
      items: [
        {
          type: `comment`,
          content: `Hi! I'm Dylan!`
        },
        {
          type: `comment`,
          content: `Hi Dylan. Nice to meet you!`
        },
        {
          type: `comment`,
          content: `Welcome to the chapter about load()!`
        }
      ]
    },
  }
}
```

This file consists only of the exported `load()` function, which returns an object containing another `notifications` object. Remember that universal `load()` functions can export anything so long as it resides inside an object. The `notifications` object is quite simple as it consists of two properties; a `count` property with the value of 3 and another property labeled `items`, which is just an array of three other objects. To show how the data isn't loaded every time we navigate to a new page, we've included a `console.log()` call that outputs the text `notifications loaded`.

Next, we'll make some changes to our root layout template so it can actually use our freshly loaded data. For the most part, it will stay the same, but we'll need to add some markup that can show the data as well as minimal styling to convey the concept of a **notification badge**:

src/routes/+layout.svelte

```
<script>
  import Nav from '$lib/Nav.svelte';
  import Notify from '$lib/Notify.svelte';

  export let data;
</script>
<div class='wrapper'>
  <div class='nav'>
    <div class='menu'>
      <Nav />
    </div>
    <div class='notifications'>
      <Notify count={data.notifications.count}/>
    </div>
  </div>
  <div class='content'>
    <slot></slot>
  </div>
  <div class='footer'>
    This is my footer
  </div>
</div>
<style>
  .wrapper {
    min-height: 100vh;
    display: grid;
    grid-template-rows: auto 1fr auto;
  }
  .footer {
    text-align: center;
```

```
    margin: 20px 0;
  }
  .nav {
    text-align: center;
  }
  .menu {
    display: inline-block;
  }
  .notifications {
    float: right;


  }
</style>
```

Here are some important changes to make note of in this version of +layout.svelte:

- A new Notify component is imported (shown next).

- We exported the data variable to make use of the data returned from src/routes/+layout.js.

- The notifications count property is sent to the Notify component.

- The markup for the .menu and .notifications elements are added to the .nav div element. This allows us to show the Notify component in the top-right corner of the page.

- New styles for elements with the .nav, .menu, and .notifications classes are added to style our new markup.

Next, let's look at the Notify component we just imported. This component will contain the markup that shows our notification count and links to the /notification route:

src/lib/Notify.svelte

```
<script>
  export let count = 0;
</script>
<a href='/notifications'>
  {count}
</a>
<style>
  a {
    padding: 15px;
    color: white;
```

```
    text-decoration: none;
    background-color: #ea6262;
  }
</style>
```

This component is relatively simple. Firstly, it exports the count variable and gives it a default value of 0. This is necessary because, while this component is used inside the layout, it does not exist underneath or alongside the +layout.js file we created earlier and so it does not have access to the information provided by the layout load() function. Next, this component creates a link tag to contain the count variable. And finally, it contains spartan styling to decorate our notification badge.

Finally, let's look at the notifications page. Because this file exists underneath the hierarchy of +layout. js, we can access data as if it were loaded from a +page.js file that existed alongside it:

src/routes/notifications/+page.svelte

```
<script>
  export let data;
</script>
{#if data.notifications.count > 0}
  <ul>
  {#each data.notifications.items as item}
    <li>{item.content}</li>
  {/each}
  </ul>
{/if}
```

This page makes use of Svelte directives: {#if} and {#each}. Since we exported the data variable at the top of the component, we can use data loaded from src/routes/+layout.js within this component. If the count property of the notifications objects is greater than zero, it will create the markup necessary for an unordered list. It then outputs the content property of each comment item inside a list item.

Now, when you open your project in your browser, you should see a new notification badge displayed in the top-right corner of the app showing the value of the count property from the notification object. Try selecting some of the items in the navigation menu and see how the text **notifications loaded** isn't output every time you click a link. It is shown on the initial load in both the development server as well as the browser console but not run again. That is because the data being loaded has yet to change, and SvelteKit recognizes this.

Let's look at forcing the data to be reloaded when we click on the notification badge. We can do this by using `invalidateAll` imported from `$app/navigation`. If the `load()` function used `fetch()`, it would make sense to use the `invalidate` module instead. In that instance, we would force the reload by passing the URL specified inside of the `fetch()` call to `invalidate()`. Since we're simply returning an object, we'll need to use `invalidateAll()` to trigger the reload:

src/lib/Notify.svelte

```
<script>
  import { invalidateAll } from '$app/navigation';
  export let count = 0;
</script>
<a href='/notifications' on:click={() => invalidateAll()}>
  {count}
</a>
```

In the `Notify.svelte` component, we've added the import of `invalidateAll`. When the notification link badge is clicked, it calls `invalidateAll()`, informing SvelteKit to rerun all `load()` functions within the context. Now, when you click the notification link at the top of the page, you should see the browser console output **notifications loaded**. Navigating to other pages such as **About**, **News**, or **Home** will not produce the output.

In the future, should you find yourself building components that will be showing dynamic data across an application's interface, consider the concepts we've just covered. By loading data in layout files, you can reduce the number of HTTP requests or database queries made, which can significantly improve the experience of the application for your users. And should you need to force that data to be reloaded, you'll know how to go about invalidating data so SvelteKit will re-run the appropriate `load()` functions. Next, let's take a look at how `load()` can be leveraged further to build more advanced functionality.

Destructuring RequestEvent

When it comes to `load()`, the server seems to have more information available to it than the client does. With so much data, it can be hard to know exactly all the information that is available. In short, server `load()` functions are called with a SvelteKit-specific `RequestEvent`. Here's a quick breakdown of the properties (`prop`) and functions (`fn`) available from that object:

- `cookies` (`prop`) – The cookies sent during the request.
- `fetch` (`fn`) – A compatible variant of the Web API `fetch()` function discussed in *Chapter 3*. It comes with the added benefit of allowing requests based on relative routes as well as passing cookies and headers through when on the same server.
- `getClientAddress` (`fn`) – Returns the client's IP address.

- `locals` (prop) – Any custom data inserted into the request via SvelteKit's `handle()` hook. We'll cover that in a later chapter.

- `params` (prop) – Parameters specific to the current route, such as the article slug passed to the news example in the previous chapter.

- `platform` (prop) – Data added by the environment adapter.

- `request` (prop) – The actual request data represented as an object.

- `route` (prop) – The identifier of the requested route.

- `setHeaders` (fn) – Allows for the manipulation of headers in the returned `Response` object.

- `url` (prop) – Data about the requested URL, which we covered in *Chapter 3*.

RequestEvent demo

To see this information for yourself, create the `src/routes/+layout.server.js` file with a `console.log()` function outputting a single passed-in argument to `load()`. By creating it in the root layout, you'll be able to see how properties change based on the different routes accessed from your browser. The data will then be shown in your development console.

A practical example where you may find yourself needing to utilize this data is in the case of user authentication. Normally, after a user has authenticated, they are given a cookie (*for doing such a good job entering their password – pun intended*) to store on their device, which ensures their authentication will persist for the duration of their visit. If they leave the application, it can later be used to confirm their identity so they aren't required to authenticate yet again. Let's observe how this might be accomplished with SvelteKit. Since this chapter is about `load()`, we'll build the actual form and discuss how to set the cookies in the next chapter. For now, we'll simply check whether the user has a cookie set and set one manually in the browser.

To begin, let's rename `src/routes/+layout.js` to `src/routes/+layout.server.js`. If we're going to access cookie data, we'll need access to the data provided by `RequestEvent`. By adding the logic to our root server layout, we have the added benefit of keeping the authentication checks in place across the entire application:

---

src/routes/+layout.server.js

```
export function load({ cookies }) {
  const data = {
    notifications: {
      count: 3,
      items: [
        {
          type: `comment`,
```

```
        content: `Hi! I'm Dylan!`
      },
      ...
    ]
  }
};
if(cookies.get('identity') === '1') {
  // lookup user ID in database
  data.user = {
    id: 1,
    name: 'Dylan'
  }
}
return data;
}
```

In this new version of the root layout logic, we've destructured the argument passed to load() since we currently only need access to the cookies property. We kept the notifications object we created earlier but put it inside a new variable called data. This text also omits a couple of entries for the sake of brevity. From there, we check whether the request sent to our application contained a cookie by the name of user with the value of 1. If it did, we insert some fake user information into the user property of the data object. Normally at this point, we would check the cookie value against valid sessions in a database, and if one was found, we would then retrieve the appropriate user data and send that back to the client, but we're trying to keep it simple. After all of that, the data object is returned from load().

Next, we'll need to actually show that the user has been successfully authenticated. To do this, we'll create a new route where our user can log in:

src/routes/login/+page.svelte

```
<script>
  export let data;
</script>
{#if data.user}
  <p>
    Welcome, {data.user.name}!
  </p>
{/if}
```

As we covered in the last section, the data returned from +layout.js or +layout.server.js is made available in child components by exporting the data variable. Once that is done, we use the Svelte {#if} directive to check whether we have the user property set. If found, we then display the name property of data.user.

Of course, nowhere in this example do we ever set a cookie. We'll cover that in the next chapter so, for now, let's manually create the cookie in our browser. Before doing so, navigate to the /login route and verify that nothing is shown on the page. Once you have confirmed it is a blank page, go ahead and create the cookie using the following steps for your browser:

- **Firefox**:

  I.   Open **Developer Tools** by using the *F12* key. Alternatively, open **Menu | More Tools | Developer Tools**.

  II.   In **Developer Tools**, select the tab labeled **Storage**.

  III. Under **Cookies**, select the project **URL**. Doing so should show all available cookies for the domain.

  IV.   Click the + symbol to add an item.

  V.   Double-click the **name** field and enter the text identity.

  VI.   Double-click the **value** field and enter the text 1.

  VII. Ensure the **path** field is set to / using the same steps.

- **Chrome**:

  I.   Open **Developer Tools** by using the *F12* key. Alternatively, open the **Menu | More Tools | Developer Tools**.

  II.   In **Developer Tools**, select the tab labeled **Application**.

  III. In the **Storage** section, select the **Cookies** menu item.

  IV.   Select the project URL.

  V.   In the empty windowpane, select the **name** column and enter identity.

  VI.   Select the **value** column and enter 1.

  VII. Ensure the **path** field is set to / using the same steps.

Having followed these steps, you should now have the correct cookie in your browser. After doing so, refresh the /login page in your browser and you'll see a message welcoming the user with the value from the name property specified. This example is quite simple and actual cookie-based login systems are functionally slightly more complicated; however, the concepts remain the same.

While the example we covered only made use of the cookies property from RequestEvent, we saw how trivial it would be to access any of the other properties such as url and params, or even to set our own headers with the setHeaders function. With all of that data available to us, the possibilities of what could be built into our application are nearly limitless.

Summary

In this chapter, we covered a lot of information about `load()`. We first discussed how it can be done only in the client and then moved on to some finer details about how it works. After that, we looked at using `load()` in layouts to minimize the number of requests made for each page load and maximize convenient access to data that may be needed application-wide. We also looked at invalidating data in cases where we would want data to be reloaded. Finally, we covered how server `load()` functions are called by `RequestEvent`, which gives us access to so much more valuable information. That information can enable us to build cookie-based login functionality for our application.

Having spent this chapter learning about some of the finer details behind `load()`, you should feel comfortable taking a load off and relaxing. If you have any baked cookies to hand, I suggest you take a break from the book and treat yourself to some. You've earned it.

But do come back because, in the next chapter, we'll cover more of the finer details behind receiving data from users through the use of forms, making the forms fun, and reducing the friction of data entry by utilizing snapshots.

Resources

devalue: `https://github.com/rich-harris/devalue`

6

Forms and Data Submission

In the previous chapter, we went into some of the finer details behind loading data in SvelteKit. While loading data is important, it is equally important that we understand how to empower users to submit that data. That is why this chapter will explore some of the finer details behind forms and actions in SvelteKit. While not all applications *have* to accept data from users, the ones that do so in an intuitive manner tend to rise above the rest. After all, some of the best user experiences are taken for granted because they simply work. It's when things break that users begin paying attention to them.

Throughout this chapter, we'll learn how leveraging `<form>` elements can keep our application accessible and our code minimal. Integrating those forms with easily implemented actions lets us take the submitted data and process it accordingly. And finally, we'll look at how we can soften some of the edges of the standard user experience surrounding forms by adding progressive enhancements. To do all of this, we'll put the finishing touches on the login form we started previously.

In this chapter, we'll cover the following:

- Form Setup
- Analyzing Actions
- Enhancing Forms

Upon completing this chapter, you should feel comfortable creating your very own login form, and you'll know how to go forward and accept all types of data from users of your SvelteKit-based application.

Technical requirements

The complete code for this chapter is available on GitHub at: `https://github.com/PacktPublishing/SvelteKit-Up-and-Running/tree/main/chapters/chapter06`.

Form Setup

We took a glance at using forms and actions together in *Chapter 4*. And while covering RequestEvent in the previous chapter, we began creating the code necessary to authenticate a user in our application with cookies. However, in that example, we never gave the user a means to provide a username or password. We also never created the cookie in the application. Instead, we opted to manually create one using the browser's developer tools. It's time we bring the whole thing together. Since we've covered the logic related to load(), as well as the details surrounding RequestEvent, we can continue building off of our previous example. A good place to start would be the login form itself. After all, we can't log a user in without giving them a place to do so.

But before we create the form, let's go ahead and add a link to the login page in our navigation:

src/lib/Nav.svelte

```
<nav>
  <ul>
    <li><a href='/'>Home</a></li>
    <li><a href='/news'>News</a></li>
    <li><a href='/fetch'>Fetch</a></li>
    <li><a href='/comment'>Comment</a></li>
    <li><a href='/about'>About</a></li>
    <li><a href='/api/post'>API</a></li>
    <li><a href='/login'>Login</a></li>
  </ul>
</nav>
```

The change is as simple as copying an existing <li> element and replacing the route and text inside <a>. This will make navigating and testing our login functionality simpler.

Next, let's start with the actual form. Looking back at the file we created to show users a successful login based on their cookie, we'll need to make several changes. Firstly, we'll import the enhance module from $app/forms. We'll discuss some of the magic behind this one later in this chapter, so don't worry about it for now. Next, we'll want to export the form variable so that we can signal to the user the status of their login. Finally, we'll need to create the <form> element with appropriate inputs and give it some styling:

src/routes/login/+page.svelte

```
<script>
  import { enhance } from '$app/forms';
  export let data;
  export let form;
</script>
```

```
{#if form?.msg}
  {form.msg}
{/if}
{#if data.user}
  <p>
    Welcome, {data.user.name}!
  </p>
{/if}
<form use:enhance method="POST" action="?/login">
  <label for="username">Username</label>
  <input name="username" id="username" type="text"/>
  <label for="password">Password</label>
  <input name="password" id="password" type="password"/>
  <button>Log In</button>
</form>
<style>
  form {
    display: flex;
    flex-direction: column;
    justify-content: center;
    width: 25%;
    margin: 0 auto;
  }
  input {
    margin: .25em 1em 1em;
    display: block;
  }
  label {
    margin: 0 .5em;
  }
</style>
```

Now that you've seen the additions altogether, let's discuss them. Aside from the new imports and exports, the next change you'll notice is the Svelte directive checking whether or not `form?.msg` is set. If that is set, we display the message.

data versus form

The `form` prop comes to us from the data returned by our login action (which will be created in the next section). Remember that we include `export let data;` to get access to the data prop returned from `load()`. In the same vein, we include `export let form;` to retrieve data that has been returned by form actions. The data returned can also be retrieved anywhere in the application via the `$page.form` store.

The next big change is the addition of the `<form>` element. It makes use of the `enhance` module we imported earlier, sets the HTTP method to POST, and sends its data to the `login` action located at `src/routes/login/+page.server.js`. We *must set the HTTP method to POST*; otherwise, our form will attempt to submit data via a GET request, and we don't want to be sending passwords around insecurely.

We've then included the appropriate markup for inputs, labels, and buttons. For now, we're only referencing one form action to manage logging a user in. If we wanted to enable registration or password reset functionality and keep the subsequent actions in the same file as our login action, we could leverage the `formaction` property. However, `formaction` is intended to be used when you have multiple buttons referring to separate endpoints within the same `<form>` element. In a password reset scenario, we would likely need another `<form>` element specifying the email to send our password reset link. Likewise, with registration, we would probably need to obtain a user's email, as well as their username and password, so having both of those within the context of a form that *only* accepts username and password details makes little sense. In each of these cases, it would make more sense to create a separate form for each of the features and specify the action directly on the `<form>` element. It may still make sense to keep logic concerning authentication in a single `+page.server.js` file for the sake of project organization.

The actual markup for creating a form is relatively straightforward to implement. We've just seen that we need to specify the method as well as the action to be called. And to obtain information returned from our action, we'll need to include `export let form;` on the page while making use of data returned from the action. Now that you've seen a few variations of it, you should be comfortable creating forms to accept data from your users. Of course, a form doesn't do much good if we don't make use of the submitted data. In the next section, we'll create an action to handle the data collected by the form. To ensure our action works smoothly, we'll need to set up a database and discuss some security best practices.

Analyzing Actions

In *Chapter 4*, we spent a section looking at how actions worked. Now, it's time that we took a closer look at them and how they work under the hood. But before we begin, we'll need to set up another fake database and briefly discuss security. Once we've done that, we'll finish adding logic to our application and authenticate valid users. This section will cover the following:

- Database setup

- Passwords and security

- Login action

After all of this, you'll have a general understanding of how to finally create a login form for your own SvelteKit application.

Database setup

Of course, this isn't a real database. We're going to utilize yet another JSON file that will store our user data and help us simulate looking up a user and their hashed password. It should look something like this:

src/lib/users.json

```json
[
  {
    "id": "1",
    "username": "dylan",
    "password": "$2b$10$7EakXlg...",
    "identity": "301b1118-3a11-...",
    "name": "Dylan"
  },
  {
    "id": "2",
    "username": "jimmy",
    "password": "$2b$10$3rdM9VQ...",
    "identity": "62e3e3cc-adbe-...",
    "name": "Jimmy"
  }
]
```

This file is a simple array containing two user objects and various properties related to our users. For this demonstration, the values of these properties are trivial, but the values of `identity` and `password` are of particular interest to us, as we will see in the next section. The `identity` property would normally correspond to a user session ID stored in another table. It should also utilize a unique identifier and not be easily guessable. If it were, anyone could authenticate to our application as any user by simply creating the identity cookie on their device with a valid session ID. In this example, `identity` makes use of the **Crypto Web API** to generate a random **Universally Unique Identifier** (**UUID**). The Crypto Web API should not be used for hashing passwords. For this demonstration, we'll only be using it to create a UUID that will be saved in a cookie used to authenticate a user. For your testing purposes, the value could be any unique string, but this example aims to be relatively realistic. To keep this material from diverging too far from the directive of learning SvelteKit, this is all we'll need to include for our fake user database.

Passwords and Security

Because authentication is such a common feature found in web applications, it would be a disservice to not further elaborate on how to properly implement it. And because when done improperly it can have such disastrous consequences, we'll learn how to implement it securely. While we're still not connecting to a real database and are instead storing our user passwords in a JSON file (which is highly advised against for anything other than demonstration purposes), we will observe how to properly hash passwords with another package installed via npm.

To proceed further, we'll need to install **bcrypt**. In your terminal, run the following command in the project directory:

```
npm install bcrypt
```

Once this has been done, we can generate hashes with the following code. This code will only be temporary as it will give us a convenient way to generate the hashes for our passwords as well as UUIDs for the identity property of our user objects. These can then be added to your users.json file to simulate looking up a user password from a database. We'll demonstrate login functionality to utilize it afterward:

src/routes/login/+page.server.js

```
import bcrypt from 'bcrypt';
export const actions = {
  login: async ({request}) => {
    const form = await request.formData();
    const hash = bcrypt.hashSync(form.get('password'), 10);
    console.log(hash);
    console.log(crypto.randomUUID());
  }
}
```

This +page.server.js file imports the bcrypt module we just installed with npm. It then creates the login action that our <form> element submits data to. It retrieves the form data submitted by the login form via the **FormData API** and creates a secure hash of the password provided. It also outputs a randomly generated UUID. This step could also be performed in the browser by simply entering crypto.randomUUID(); into the console of the developer tools. Upon navigating to /login in your browser, filling in the password field of the form, submitting it, and then opening the server console in your terminal, you will be able to copy the hash and the randomly generated UUID to the respective password and identity properties of each user in your users.json. In this way, you can create passwords for your users. If you're using the code in this book's GitHub repository, the hashes for each of the users were derived from the following strings:

1. **password**
2. **jimmy**

> **Note**
> It should go without saying but these are considered bad passwords. Under no circumstances should you ever attempt to use these passwords or their hashes outside of this demonstration.

While we're on the subject of security, we should take this opportunity to note some practices to avoid. It's important that we developers do not use *shared variables* to store sensitive data. To clarify, that doesn't mean to not use variables to store sensitive data. Rather, we should avoid setting a variable in a form action that could then be available in `load()`. For a bad practice example, consider a developer declaring a variable for storing chat messages at the highest scope level of a `+page.server.js` file, assigning message data to it in a form action, and then returning the same variable in the same file's `load()` function. Doing so would have the potential to allow user B to view the chat messages for user A. This spillover of data can be avoided by immediately returning the data to the page instead. These same guidelines also apply to Svelte stores. When managing data on the server, we should never set the state of a store as doing so on the server could potentially make it available to all users on that server.

Now that we know how to create hashed passwords and UUIDs, we can follow some basic best practices surrounding security. If you're ever in doubt, consult the official SvelteKit documentation. As technologies change, so too can best practices. In the next section, we'll see how can finally finish the login form by creating the action to tie it all together.

Login Action

After all of that setup, we've finally made it. We can now complete the action used by the form to log our user in and set a cookie in their browser. I'm sure you're ready by now, so let's dive into it.

Previously in this file, we created some code to generate hashes for our passwords to test against. We can do away with that code and replace it with code that will look in our database for a matching username, check the provided password against the found user's hashed password, and set a cookie on the user's device:

src/routes/login/+page.server.js

```
import bcrypt from 'bcrypt';
import users from '$lib/users.json';
export const actions = {
  login: async ({request, cookies}) => {
    const form = await request.formData();
    const exists = users.filter(user => user.username === form.
      get('username'));
    const auth = exists.filter(user => bcrypt.compareSync(form.
      get('password'), user.password));
    if(!exists.length || !auth.length) {
      return {msg: 'Invalid login!'};
```

```
    }
    cookies.set('identity', auth[0].identity, {path: '/'});
    return {msg: 'success!'}
  }
}
```

In this new version, we still import the `bcrypt` module but we've also added the import of `user.json`. We then added `cookies` to the destructured `RequestEvent` parameter. After setting up the `login` action, we get the data submitted by the `<form>` element and put it into the `form` constant. Next, we use `filter()` to check against the username of each element in the `users` array. Any matches are added to the `exists` constant. We then use `filter()` again to check the submitted password against the hashed password of every user in `exists`. If a match is found, it is added to the `auth` constant. If either `exists` or `auth` contains no items in their arrays, we return a message that the login attempt was invalid.

> **Combatting account enumeration**
>
> We should never return a message alerting the user that their username (or email) was correct but that the provided password failed. Doing so would allow malicious actors to enumerate valid accounts, essentially guessing usernames in quick succession. Once done, it becomes trivial for attackers to compile a list of valid usernames and begin brute-forcing passwords on real accounts. Since users are not well known for creating strong passwords, this could lead to account takeovers for multiple accounts. This is why we only return a message alerting the user that their login attempt failed. Whether or not their username or password was incorrect is for them to figure out.

If a user was successful in logging in, we use `cookies.set()` to send the `Set-Cookie` headers telling the client to set the `identity` cookie to the user's session ID on the root directory of the domain. We must specify the root path in the options; otherwise, our cookie will default to only working at the highest level route where it was set – in this case, only on pages such as `/login`. You can imagine how frustrating that would be for users. We can then check whether the user is authorized to access functionality at various locations across the application. To remove the same cookie and log a user out, we could use `cookies.delete()` while passing in the name of the cookie, as well as our path.

Finally, to show users whether or not their login attempt was successful, we'll need to make a couple of adjustments to our root server layout. If you recall, we previously only checked whether `identity === '1'`. With a fake database implemented, we can instead check against our user's JSON file:

src/routes/+layout.server.js

```
import users from '$lib/users.json';
export function load({ cookies }) {
  const data = {
    notifications: {
      count: 3,
      items: [...]
    }
  };
  const exists = users.filter(user => user.identity === cookies.
get('identity'));
  if(exists.length) {
    const {password, ...user} = {...exists[0]};
    data.user = user;
  }
  return data;
}
```

Since we need to check the `identity` cookie value against those that exist in `users.json`, we'll need to import it first. We don't need to change anything with the `data` constant yet, so we can leave the code related to notifications alone. We must then utilize `filter()` to find whether any users exist with the value obtained from the identity cookie and assign those found to the `exists` constant. If `exists` has values, we obtain the first one found and harness the power of a destructuring assignment to avoid passing the user's password into `data.user`. This is done to prevent including sensitive data.

Now that we've put it all together, we can verify that the login works by navigating to `/login` in our browser and typing in the appropriate details. If you have created your own hashes, you'll need to use the strings you provided to successfully authenticate. Upon submitting the form, we should be greeted by the status message, as well as the welcome message from `src/routes/login/+page.svelte`.

To recap, in this section, we created a fake user database using a JSON file. We included our secure password hashes in that file to check against. When a username and password are submitted from the `<form>` element in `src/routes/login/+page.svelte`, that data is retrieved using the **FormData API** in the login action located at `src/routes/login/+page.server.js`. We then checked for the username as well as that user's hashed password; if found, we send the `Set-Cookie` headers in our response by way of `cookies.set()` and send a *Success* status message. If a login attempt does not match a username or password, we return an *Invalid Login* status message. Now that we know how to create a form and submit our data to the appropriate actions, let's examine some methods that can improve the user experience of our application.

Enhancing Forms

To reduce the friction inherent in forms on the web, SvelteKit provides us with a few options. We saw the first of those options earlier when we set use:enhance on our login form. This one is great for keeping the page from redirecting as it can submit the form data in the background, which means our page doesn't need to be reloaded. Another tool we've yet to see is what SvelteKit calls **snapshots**. In this section, we'll look at both and how they can help improve the experience of your application:

- enhance
- Snapshots

After completing this section, you'll be capable of building forms for your users that will be intuitive and streamlined, leading to far greater chances of acceptance by users of your application.

enhance

By importing enhance from $app/forms, we can progressively enhance the flow of <form> elements. This means that we can submit the data without requiring a page reload, which would normally be found when submitting an <form> element. We've seen this action a couple of times now but in both cases we never discussed how it works.

The first step that's taken by enhance is updating the form property. We were able to observe this with the Svelte directive located in src/routes/login/+page.svelte, which checks whether form?.msg is set. Because Svelte is reactive, when enhance updates form, we can immediately view the change and display our message. enhance will also update $page.form and $page.status, which are both properties of the Svelte $page store. This store gives us information about the currently displayed page. $page.form will contain the same data returned from the form action, whereas $page.status will contain HTTP status code data. We first saw an example of the $page store used in the *Dynamic routing* section of *Chapter 4*.

Upon receiving a successful response, enhance will reset the <form> element and force the appropriate load() functions to rerun by calling invalidateAll(). It will then resolve any redirects, render the nearest +error.svelte (if an error occurred), and reset the focus to the correct element as if the page was being loaded for the first time.

Should enhance be used on a <form> element with an action to an entirely different route, enhance **will not update** form or $page. This is because it aims to emulate native browser behavior and submission of data across routes like this would normally trigger a page reload. To force it to update these properties, you will need to pass a callback function to enhance. The callback function can then use applyAction to update the stores accordingly. The applyAction() function accepts a SvelteKit ActionResult type and can also be imported from $app/forms.

Snapshots

One commonly frustrating experience endured by users is caused by navigating away from a page after filling out a large form but before that form has been submitted. No matter the cause, losing data that took significant time to enter is painful.

By persisting `<form>` data in a snapshot, we can make it easier for users to pick up where they left off. Fewer headaches for users means a better experience with our application. And implementing it is a breeze as we only need to export a `snapshot` constant with the `capture` and `restore` properties set. To see it in action, let's persist the comment form data we built earlier:

src/routes/comment/+page.svelte

```
<script>
  import { enhance } from '$app/forms';
  export let form;
  let comment = '';
  export const snapshot = {
    capture: () => comment,
    restore: (item) => comment = item
  }
</script>
<div class='wrap'>
  {#if form && form.status === true}
    <p>{form.msg}</p>
  {/if}
  <form method='POST' action='?/create' use:enhance>
    <label>
      Comment
      <input name="comment" type="text" bind:value={comment}>
    </label>
    <button>Submit</button>
    <button formaction='?/star'>Star</button>
    <button formaction='?/reply'>Reply</button>
  </form>
</div>
```

In this new version, we've only made three significant changes:

1. Added `let comment = '';` so that we may capture and restore the input value to our JS.

2. Added the snapshot object with `export const snapshot:`

    A. The `capture` property calls an anonymous function just before the page updates when navigating away. This function only needs to return the values we wish to capture and restore later – in this case, the value associated with `comment`.

    B. `restore` is called immediately after the page is loaded and assigns the parameter it was called with to `comment`.

3. We bind the value of the comment's `<text>` input to the `comment` variable so that the input's value may be retrieved on capture and set on restore.

Once you have implemented these changes, you can test them out by opening the `/comment` route in your browser, typing in a test comment, and navigating away to another page. When you click *Back* in your browser, you will observe the data that was restored just as you left it. Because snapshots persist the data they capture to Session Storage, you can open your browser developer tools and observe the data. In Firefox, you can find it under **Storage | Session Storage**. In Chrome, it can be located under **Application | Storage | Session Storage**. In both Chrome and Firefox, you will need to refresh the page manually to view the changed data as the developer console windowpanes will not update during client-side navigation. Because Session Storage is meant to only contain small amounts of data, anything saved here must be serialized into JSON. It is worth noting that the data will only be restored upon navigating *Back* to the page. SvelteKit will only trigger the restore based on browser history. Navigating to the `/comment` page by clicking the link in the menu will not trigger a restore as it is considered navigating to a new page.

Knowing how to progressively and seamlessly enhance your forms can lead to an experience that will keep users coming back. By running form submissions in the background, we can make use of Svelte's reactivity to provide immediate and useful feedback to users. And with the use of snapshots, we can preserve a user's progress on simple or complex forms. With this knowledge, you can now go forth and build intuitive experiences into your applications.

Summary

We started this chapter by building a simple `<form>` element that accepts a username and password. On the same page component, we relayed the status of the authentication attempt back to the user. After this, we created a form action that looked up the username and compared the provided password with a hashed value. If successful, we logged the user in by setting a cookie on their device. If unsuccessful, we informed the user that their attempt had failed. We also briefly discussed some security best practices surrounding authenticating users with our application. We then examined how experiences with `<form>` elements can be improved by using `enhance` and snapshots. Having done all of this, we can be confident in any forms we implement in future SvelteKit projects.

With everything we've covered up until this point, you should be able to put together a basic website or application. In the next chapter, we'll cover more advanced functionality that can truly showcase the power of building with SvelteKit. We will look at even more advanced routing concepts noting how they've made use of features we've already discussed and explaining some that have yet to be covered.

Resources

The following are the resources for this chapter:

- bcrypt: `https://github.com/kelektiv/node.bcrypt.js`
- Crypto Web API: `https://developer.mozilla.org/en-US/docs/Web/API/Crypto`

7

Advanced Routing Techniques

With everything we've covered so far, you could set this book down now and go build a simple website using SvelteKit. But if you wanted to build more advanced functionality into your application, you might find yourself struggling to come up with the proper hierarchies for routes. That's because when it comes to dynamic routing, we've only scratched the surface. In *Chapter 4*, we discussed creating dynamic pages with parameters passed to our routes. In that example, we loaded articles by using the provided slug and matching it with those found in our demonstration database. We had no way of knowing what the slug would be ahead of time and it would have been needlessly complicated to create a new route for each article. Instead, we looked at the slug parameter that was received based on the URL being accessed.

This was only a brief introduction to dynamic routing. In this chapter, we'll look at some more advanced techniques that can help you supercharge your routing logic. We'll examine routing with optional parameters, parameters of unknown lengths, how to match parameters with regular expressions, which routes will take precedence in instances of routing logic collisions, and more advanced layout techniques, including methodologies for breaking out of them.

This chapter will be broken into the following topics:

- Using optional parameters
- Rest parameters
- Matching, sorting, and encoding – oh, my!
- Advanced layouts

By the end of this chapter, you will have a mastery of the various routing techniques available to you in SvelteKit. No matter your next SvelteKit project's requirements, you will have the knowledge required for solving and tackling any complex routing dilemmas.

Technical requirements

The complete code for this chapter is available on GitHub at: `https://github.com/PacktPublishing/SvelteKit-Up-and-Running/tree/main/chapters/chapter07`

Using optional parameters

Since we teased optional parameters in the *Creating Dynamic Pages* section of *Chapter 4*, let's start there. When creating optional parameters in a route, there are some things to keep in mind. For instance, they cannot exist alongside another route as this would cause a collision in the routing rules. When creating an optional route, it works best for instances where the final portion of the route can have a default option. Many applications will change the URL based on a language selected by the user. For our example, we'll illustrate how to create an optional parameter by selecting a country in North America that our demonstration store operates in. We won't actually build an entire store but rather use it to illustrate the advanced routing concepts in this chapter.

To begin, let's create a new route in our navigation just like we have for previous examples:

src/lib/Nav.svelte

```
<nav>
  <ul>
    <li><a href='/'>Home</a></li>
    ...
    <li><a href='/login'>Login</a></li>
    <li><a href='/store'>Store</a></li>
  </ul>
</nav>
```

All we need to do is add another list item with a link to our new route in the navigation menu. After doing that, we can create the `store` directory, which is where all of the examples for this chapter will exist:

src/routes/store/+layout.svelte

```
<h2>Store</h2>
<ul>
  <li><a href="/store/locations/">Locations</a></li>
  <li><a href="/store/products/">Products</a></li>
</ul>
<slot />
```

This simple layout will allow us to navigate the various concepts covered in this chapter. After adding links, we use the Svelte `<slot>` element referenced in earlier chapters. Take a moment to go and create all of the necessary directories. Next, we'll also create a simple landing page for the `/store` route:

src/routes/store/+page.svelte

```
<h3>Welcome to the Store!</h3>
```

Having created the files necessary for the `/store` route as well as the `locations` directory, we'll now create yet another directory. The major difference with this one will be that it uses double square brackets (`[[country]]`) in the name. This is how SvelteKit differentiates optional routes from those that are not. Because we're creating a page with an optional parameter, we don't need to create a `+page.svelte` inside of the `locations` directory. Rather, we'll add that inside of the `[[country]]` directory. To proceed, we'll create the appropriate `+page.svelte` and `+page.js` files:

src/routes/store/locations/[[country]]/+page.svelte

```
<script>
  export let data;
</script>
<h2>You're viewing the {data.country.toUpperCase()} store.</h2>
<ul>
  <li><a href="/store/locations">North America</a></li>
  <li><a href="/store/locations/ca">Canada</a></li>
  <li><a href="/store/locations/me">Mexico</a></li>
  <li><a href="/store/locations/us">United States</a></li>
</ul>
```

By now, this should look all too familiar. We use `export let data;` so that we may access the information provided by `load()` in the next file. We use that data to inform the user which country's store locations they are viewing and display the abbreviation in uppercase. We then create an unordered list populated with links to the various allowed routes we will provide in the next file.

In `[[country]]/+page.js`, we need to check the provided parameters of the route against the list of countries our store operates in. We can do so with the following code:

src/routes/store/locations/[[country]]/+page.js

```
export function load({ params }) {
  const codes = [
    'na',
    'ca',
    'me',
    'us'
```

```
    ];
    const found = codes.filter(country_code => country_code === params.
country);
    return {country: found[0] ?? 'na'};
}
```

Exporting `load()` functions should also feel familiar to you at this point. In this particular function, we only need access to `params` and so we destructure the `RequestEvent` object passed to `load()`. We've then declared a `codes` array that works as a list of approved routes. On the next line, we check if the provided route is in the array of approved routes by running `filter()` on `codes`. Then `filter()` returns an array containing all of the matches and assigns it to the `found` constant. We can then return an object containing the `country` property, which is assigned the first value inside of `found`. If the first value of `found` is empty, we'll default to the value that shows all of North America. In this case, `na`.

Once we've done all of this, we can open our application, click **store**, click **locations**, and view the various North American countries our store operates in. When clicking each of the options from the unordered list, notice how the text on our page changes as well as the route in the URL. When we select **North America**, the text shown reflects the abbreviation **NA** due to the ternary logic used in the return of `load()`. When selecting any of the other options, the abbreviation is updated accordingly. As mentioned previously, optional parameters work best when the final section of the route can have a default option. If the optional parameter were to be included somewhere in the middle of the route, then any subsequent portions of the route would be understood by the routing mechanism as the optional parameter.

In this example, we created a new route using double square brackets `[[ ]]`. While this example has a long way to go before functioning as a complete store, it should illuminate how to use optional parameters in routes. Now that you understand optional parameters, let's see how we can wrangle routes of unknown lengths.

Rest parameters

Just as JavaScript functions can accept rest parameters using the rest operator (…), so too can our routes. By using a rest operator inside of single square brackets, we can allow a variable length on the specified route. This feature comes in handy when creating something like a file browser where the URL should match a path that then makes the page content shareable via the URL.

To see this concept in action, let's create a `products` route in our store. Start by adding `src/routes/store/products/+layout.svelte` so that we may navigate products easily:

src/routes/store/products/+layout.svelte

```
<h3>Products</h3>
<ul>
  <li><a href="/store/products/shirts">Shirts</a></li>
```

```
<li><a href="/store/products/shirts/mens">Mens Shirts</a></li>
<li><a href="/store/products/shirts/mens/tshirts">Men's T-shirts
  </a></li>
<li><a href="/store/products/shirts/mens/tshirts/cotton">Men's
  Cotton T-shirts</a></li>
<li><a href="/store/products/shirts/mens/tshirts/cotton/
  graphic">Men's Graphic Cotton T-shirts</a></li>
</ul>
<slot />
```

This Svelte component is rather simple. It consists of a title, an unordered list, list items, and links to various products. Again, we've used the Svelte `<slot />` element to keep the navigation on our page as we click around. Next, let's create an endpoint that can handle the varying lengths of products we've just provided. To do so, we'll create a folder using square brackets and prefix the directory name with the rest operator. For this example, we'll use `[...details]` as the directory name. Let's look at the +page.js and +page.svelte files now:

src/routes/store/products/[...details]/+page.js

```
export function load({ params }) {
  return params;
}
```

Since we're not building out an entire store, we can keep this one incredibly simple. As we're attempting to showcase how rest parameters work within SvelteKit's routing mechanism, we'll simply return params from load(). A more robust and practical example might take the value from params and use it to filter a list of products retrieved from the database. That data could then be returned from load() for each product to be rendered in the next file.

Now, to show how the rest parameter value changes, we'll add the following +page.svelte:

src/routes/store/products/[...details]/+page.svelte

```
<script>
  export let data;
</script>
<h4>Product page</h4>
{#if data.details}
  <p class='red'>{data.details}</p>
{:else}
  <p>No product selected! Try clicking one or adding your own URL.
{/if}

<style>
```

```
    .red {
      color: red;
      font-weight: bold;
    }
  </style>
```

Again, we're keeping things simple. Instead of showing all of the products that could be available in data, we're simply using the Svelte {#if} and {:else} directives to demonstrate how the details parameter changes. If data.details is empty, we show a default message. If it has a value, we show it in bold red text. Had we given the directory a different name, that name would be how we accessed the parameter. Try clicking some of the links to the various products and notice how the URL changes in the browser but so too does the value in red. What happens if you add your own values to the URL after /store/products/?

With these advanced routing techniques, we have to consider some implications. For instance, just as optional parameters work best when at the end section of the URL, rest parameters cannot be followed by an optional parameter. If we attempt to provide optional routing sections after the rest parameter, they will be consumed by the rest parameter. To see the error thrown by the Vite development server, try creating an optional directory inside of /[...details]/. You won't have to worry about accidentally doing this since Vite will be watching out for you, but it's still good to know about it when planning routes for your application.

If you find yourself building routes of an unknown length into your application, consider creating them using SvelteKit's rest parameters. Not only do they handle those indeterminate lengths, but the logic is easily incorporated into the existing flow of SvelteKit apps.

Matching, sorting, and encoding – oh, my!

If you're unfamiliar with the ins and outs of SvelteKit's more advanced routing techniques, it can quickly become unwieldy. To get ahead of the unexpected, we're going to look at a few more strategies you can use to ensure your application's routing works as you intend it to. In this section, we will cover how you can ensure that parameters are of the type you're expecting them to be. We'll then examine how SvelteKit handles URLs that can resolve to multiple routes. We'll wrap it up with a bit of information about encoding URLs. You can expect to see the following sub-sections:

- Matching
- Sorting
- Encoding

Once finished, you'll be one step closer to mastering the routing of SvelteKit apps.

Matching

We've looked at how we can use optional and rest parameters in our routes. But think back to the example we created in *Chapter 4* dealing with dynamic routes. In the news section, we only checked whether the provided [slug] parameter existed in our database. If we wanted to ensure that the value being passed to our database was in fact a slug, we could create a custom matcher to do just that.

To create a matcher with SvelteKit, we add a JS file with a descriptive name to src/params/. If the directory doesn't exist yet, don't fret! You can simply go ahead and create it now. The files here export a single function: match(). That function accepts one string parameter and returns a boolean value. Because the value passed to the function is a string, we'll use **regular expressions** (**regex**) to ensure the parameter passed in is of the type we want enforced on our route. Regex may seem daunting at first but there exist plenty of tools online to assist in the creation and learning of regex rules. See the end of this chapter for more resources. Now let's create a matcher for our news articles to ensure they are being passed a proper slug before we perform our database lookup:

src/params/slug.js

```js
export function match(str) {
   return /^[a-z0-9]+(?:-[a-z0-9]+)*$/gim.test(str);
}
```

As is clear, matchers need not be overly complicated. It simply needs to export the match() function, which accepts a string parameter. This matcher then tests that string against a regex literal, returning true for a match and false for a mismatch. This regex tests for one or more string or number characters followed by a – character, which must be followed by one or more string or number characters. A string ending with a – character is considered invalid.

> **Applying matchers**
>
> When applying a matcher to a specific route, the value following the = character is the name of the given matcher. Another example may include creating a matcher that tests for integers. That rule could be enforced on a dynamic route by setting the parameter like so: [param=integer] where params/integer.js is the name of the matcher file.

To apply the matcher we just created to our news articles, we need to rename src/routes/news/[slug] to src/routes/news/[slug=slug]. Once we have adjusted the parameter in our route accordingly, we can go back and view our news articles just as we did before. Of course, the existing articles will match just fine as they contain valid slugs. To test that this matcher is being applied before we run our database lookup, we can create a new article in src/lib/articles.json. The content and title of the new article object are irrelevant but by creating an article with an invalid slug, we can confirm the matcher is working. Once you have created an article with a bad slug, attempt to view it. You should receive a **404 Not Found** error even though the article exists. This is because the dynamic parameter passed in did not match our provided regular expression.

While regular expressions can be intimidating to work with, it's comforting to know that SvelteKit empowers developers to harness the power behind them. Being able to do so ensures our applications work as we intend them to. However, there may still be instances where SvelteKit routes to an endpoint in an unexpected way. To avoid these situations, let's take a look at which routing rules take precedence over others.

Sorting

Since it is entirely possible for a URL to match multiple routes, it's important to understand which routing rules will be executed in which order. Similar to how CSS rules are given different weights, so too are the rules in SvelteKit's routing. So which routing rules will be executed when and how do we avoid collisions?

1. More specific routes will always take precedence over less specific routes. A route without a parameter is considered the highest level. For example, `src/routes/about/+page.svelte` will be executed before `src/routes/[param]/+page.svelte`.

2. Applying a matcher to a dynamic parameter will give it a higher priority than those without a matcher. Calling `src/routes/news/[slug=slug]/+page.svelte` will be given priority over `src/routes/news/[slug]/+page.svelte`.

3. Optional and rest parameters are given the least preference. If they are not the final section of the route, they are ignored. For instance, `src/routes/[x]/+page.svelte` will execute before `src/routes/[...rest]/+page.svelte`.

4. Tiebreakers are determined by alphabetical order of the parameters. That is, `src/routes/[x]/+page.svelte` will execute before `src/routes/[z]/+page.svelte`.

If you're planning to leverage the more advanced routing features of SvelteKit, then understanding these rules is an absolute must. Try customizing the routes created in your project and adjusting them to create collisions. See if you can resolve the collisions yourself or predict which pages will be called before others. Next, we'll look at how to manage special characters in URLs via encoding.

Encoding

At some point in their career, every developer has encountered issues with encoding, yet no one ever takes the time to fully understand them. Since you're a busy developer, eager to get started building, and you probably didn't pick up this book to get lectured about encoding, we'll keep this short. To prevent serious frustration when building routes that make use of special characters, SvelteKit lets us encode the routes so they may be used in URLs. Of course, some characters such as [ ] ( ) # and % have special meanings either in SvelteKit or the browser and so they are mostly off limits. However, they can still be used when properly encoded in the routing mechanism and URL encoded for the browser.

When creating routes with special characters in SvelteKit, the special characters are written inside of square brackets `[ ]` similar to how dynamic parameters are. However, they are then prefixed by `x+` and followed by the hexadecimal value of the character. An example of this is when creating a route to the `/.well-known/` directory, which could be represented like so: `src/routes/[x+2e]well-known/+page.svelte`. In most cases, there should be no issues with this route and encoding won't be necessary, but we're using it for demonstration purposes. Go ahead and create it in your project. In the browser, navigate to the development site and append the `/.well-known/` route to confirm it works. Now try to create the route `/?-help/`. Because `?` is a special character in the browser, it must be encoded to properly execute. We can create the route using the hexadecimal values like this: `src/routes/[x+3f]-help/+page.svelte`. But we won't be able to access the web page at `/?-help/`. Instead, we'll need to access that particular route at `/%3f%-help/`. Whenever using a special character in routes, consider encoding it with the hexadecimal values beforehand.

To obtain the hexadecimal value of a character, you can use the following JS snippet: `':'.charCodeAt(0).toString(16);` where `:` is the special character you'd like to retrieve the hexadecimal value for. We're not limited to only using hexadecimal values for simple text either. SvelteKit's routing also supports **Unicode** standards. As such, we could use an emoji directly within our routes. If we needed to work around encoding with Unicode, we could use `[u+xxxx]` where `xxxx` is the Unicode code point.

To ensure our application behaves as expected, it's essential to know how to properly encode special characters. We also looked at how we can apply matchers to routes so that we can ensure dynamic parameters are of the type we're expecting them to be. And with our cursory glance at how routes are given precedence over others, you should feel comfortable exploring even more advanced techniques in your application's routing.

Advanced layouts

The more complex the application, the more complex the structure becomes. To keep application logic organized we can utilize more advanced routing mechanisms such as layout groups and breakouts. By using layout groups, we can organize various layout components without cluttering the application URL. And by inserting simple syntax into pages and templates, we can break a layout or page out from its hierarchy while keeping the structure of our application intact.

Since we organize our application components into logical groupings, it makes sense to organize application functionality into logical groupings as well. To demonstrate using a real-world example, consider interface components that are available to logged-in users but not available to anonymous users. When logged in, users can interact with other users through comments, change their profile information, or view their own notifications. A user of the site that is not logged in should not see any of these components. With what we've learned so far about layouts, creating different layouts for each type of user could potentially run us into the issue of affecting our application's clean URL. This is where we can harness SvelteKit's layout groups.

When creating a layout group, use parenthesis ( ) to surround the directory name. All content inside of that layout group will then be included in the group and slotted in the +layout.svelte file found there. To demonstrate layout groups, we'll create two groups: (app) and (site). Inside of (app), we'll move logic related to the application features, and inside of (site), we'll move logic commonly found in basic websites. Our new routes directory structure should look similar to this:

src/routes/

```
src/
|_routes/
   |_(app)/
   |   |_comment/
   |   |_login/
   |   |_notifications/
   |   |_store/
   |
   |_(site)/
   |   |_about/
   |   |_fetch/
   |   |_news/
   |
   |_api/
   |_+layout.server.js
   |_+layout.svelte
   |_+page.svelte
```

After shuffling our folders around, we can create a layout for each of our new layout groups:

src/routes/(app)/+layout.svelte

```
<div class='app_layout'>
  <slot />
</div>
<style>
  .app_layout {
    background: #cac4c4;
    padding: 1rem;
  }
</style>
```

In this layout file, we're wrapping all of the content that will be rendered in the Svelte `<slot />` directive with another `<div>` element that will apply a background color. For simplicity's sake, we're only attempting to demonstrate how different layout groups work. The next file does exactly the same thing but applies a different color:

src/routes/(site)/+layout.svelte

```
<div class='site_layout'>
  <slot />
</div>
<style>
  .site_layout {
    background: #83a8ee;
    padding: 1rem;
  }
</style>
```

After saving these layouts, you'll notice the application shows different background colors when navigating the browser to `comment/`, `login/`, `notifications/`, and `store/` than it does for `about/`, `fetch/`, and `news/`. However, our URLs remain exactly the same!

For cases where want to break a particular layout or page out of the existing hierarchy, we can append the @ character to the filename. For example, `+page@` or `+layout@`. We can then follow it up with the name of the directory we would like it to inherit directly from. If no name is provided after the @ character, then the root layout will be utilized. We can see this in action by renaming `src/routes/(app)/store/products/[...details]/+page.svelte` to `src/routes/(app)/store/products/[...details]/+page@(app).svelte`. Doing so moves the product page out of the product and store layouts. Try renaming it to `+page@store.svelte` to keep the store layout or `+page@.svelte` to take it all the way back to the root layout. Of course, our product links are no longer visible as the markup to show them was included in `src/routes/(app)/store/products/+layout.svelte`, but we're only trying to demonstrate how you can break a page out of its immediate layouts. This functionality can be useful for separating your application logic into administrative or authenticated sections while keeping the URL unaffected.

We've just seen how we can break out of layouts using @ symbols in the Svelte component naming conventions. When we include @ followed by the name of our desired layout, the file will inherit directly from the named layout instead of all layouts between. We've also seen how we can create layout groups to keep our project structured without disrupting the application URL. With everything we've covered, you should be capable of meeting even the most complex routing requirements for any SvelteKit project.

Summary

In the chapters leading up to this, we covered core routing concepts. In this chapter, we looked at the more advanced techniques available in SvelteKit. These techniques can help us further customize our application and address edge cases. When it comes to routing, we now have an understanding of how we can create optional parameters with default values. We've also seen how rest parameters can be used to create a shareable URL of unknown lengths. Matching was shown to be useful for ensuring our application is receiving parameters of the expected types. We also saw how SvelteKit prioritizes certain routing rules over others, which is helpful for understanding the order of execution when a URL matches multiple routes. After covering how to encode special characters in routes, we looked at how we can create layout groups and even break out of the layout hierarchies while keeping application logic intact. If you've finished this chapter and feel comfortable with everything learned, you'll be able to handle even the strangest of edge cases encountered while building the routing of your SvelteKit application.

In the next chapter, we'll take a short break from routing to analyze various SvelteKit adapters and the environments they are used in. We'll also take a closer look at page options and attempt to build our application for a production environment for the first time.

Resources

- RegExr – a great site for practicing and learning regex: `https://regexr.com/`
- Unicode standards: `https://www.unicode.org/standard/standard.html`
- Programming with Unicode: `https://unicodebook.readthedocs.io/index.html`

Part 3 – Supplemental Concepts

This part aims to cover the additional requisite concepts of SvelteKit. It begins by showing you how to produce a build for a production environment with resources showing how easily it can be done using SvelteKit's adapter system. It then covers how hooks can be used to manipulate data flowing in and out of a SvelteKit application. From there, it addresses how to best import static assets by leveraging Vite. Then, it explains the various modules available in SvelteKit that make the entire framework possible. The section then covers how to ensure that a SvelteKit application can be made available to as many users as possible while boosting search engine rankings. Finally, it wraps up with various resources that will prove invaluable to any developer attempting to power their next project with SvelteKit.

This part has the following chapters:

- *Chapter 8, Builds and Adapters*
- *Chapter 9, Hooks and Error Handling*
- *Chapter 10, Managing Static Assets*
- *Chapter 11, Modules and Secrets*
- *Chapter 12, Enhancing Accessibility and Optimizing SEO*
- *Appendix Examples and Support*

8
Builds and Adapters

In the previous four chapters, we've spent a significant amount of time discussing various routing techniques. From simple routing to pages that can be rendered as static HTML and speed up our application, to more complex tactics where we ensure the data is of an expected type through the use of regular expressions. While these techniques represent core features of SvelteKit, they are not all there is to it. Another useful quality found in SvelteKit is its ability to run in nearly any environment through the use of adapters. Before we dive into various adapters and their configurations, we'll analyze the process involved when creating a production build of a SvelteKit application.

Firstly, we'll need to address how to build our application for a production environment. Vite makes this step simple, so we'll then pivot to how we can use different adapters to adjust builds for various environments. While each adapter has its own requirements, it would quickly become repetitive to discuss them all. Instead, we'll focus on three different adapters that are each suited to unique environments.

In this chapter, we will cover the following topics:

- Creating a Build
- Adapting the App

Once complete, you'll be able to build and deploy your very own applications to a multitude of platform types, including static hosts, Node.js, and a plethora of serverless environments.

Technical requirements

The complete code for this chapter is available on GitHub at: `https://github.com/PacktPublishing/SvelteKit-Up-and-Running/tree/main/chapters/chapter08`.

Creating a Build

In other books about web development frameworks, a section related to creating a production build of the application usually doesn't come until the very end. But because SvelteKit and Vite make it so simple, there's really no reason to wait. I'm sure you're eager to get your application available as soon as possible, so let's get straight to it.

So far, we've only worked with our application in the development environment. In essence, Vite started a development server on the local machine when we ran the `npm run dev` command. To shut down the development server, we use *Ctrl + C*. To prepare a production build of our application, we can use the provided npm script:

```
npm run build
```

If you open the project's `package.json`, you'll notice this particular script runs the `vite build` command. It does exactly what it sounds like by kicking off Vite's build process, which involves the bundling process from Rollup, packaging static assets, and running the configured adapter. Upon completion of the command, you'll notice the output in your terminal lists various files as well as their size. If there are any errors in the build, they will be shown here.

By default, the fully built application will be output to `.svelte-kit/`. To change this directory, we can open `svelte.config.js` and pass in the preferred directory name to the `config.kit.outDir` option. When opening the `build` folder, you'll notice that the built application has a different structure compared to our source code. This is, of course, by design and varies based on the adapter we're using. To confirm that our production build works, we can preview it using the following command:

```
npm run preview
```

Once run, Vite will alert us to the new URL and port that our application can be accessed from. We can view and use the application there just as we can when running our development server. What differs is that file changes will not be automatically updated, as the files being used to run this version of the application need to be regenerated on each build – that is, unless `build.watch` has been set in the `vite.config.js` project.

Having run the first official build of our application, there are a few things to make note of before we begin discussing adapters. Firstly, think back to *Chapter 4* when we covered **Page Options**. In that section, we looked at how we can specify server-side rendering, client-side rendering, and prerendering on a per-route basis. We can also apply those options to layouts. In fact, if we intended to create a single-page application, we would achieve it by disabling `ssr` in the root `+layout.js` file. Just keep in mind that prerendering takes place during the build of the application. As such, any `fetch()` requests that happen on prerendered pages will happen at build time. We can confirm this with a simple change to our `fetch` example. Where we previously set `ssr = false`, change it now to `prerender = true;`:

src/routes/(site)/fetch/+page.js

```
const key = 'DEMO_KEY'; // your API key here
export const prerender = true; // change this line
export function load() {
   const pic = fetch(`https://api.nasa.gov/planetary/apod?api_
key=${key}`)
     .then(response => {
       console.log('got response');
       return response.json();
     });
   return {pic};
}
```

Once we've enabled prerendering on this particular route, we can go ahead and rebuild the application. Now, when we open our `build` folder, we should see the file at the `.svelte-kit/output/prerendered/pages/fetch.html` path. Upon opening this file, we'll see the image element as well as all of the other data pulled from the NASA API shown as static HTML. This confirms to us that prerendering happens during the build process. It is very much something developers need to be cognizant of when preparing their applications for production environments.

There are a few other idiosyncrasies to take note of when building your application:

- Disabling `csr` and `ssr` will result in an empty page being rendered.

- It is not possible to prerender pages that rely on form actions as the page relies on HTTP POST requests.

- It is also not possible to prerender pages that make use of `url.searchParams`.

- It is possible to prerender pages that load data based on dynamic parameters in the route; however, SvelteKit will need to observe links to those endpoints to do so.

As demonstrated, preparing an application for production is quite simple. Vite bundles dependencies quickly and even provides a means to preview the application. That being said, there are a few things to keep in mind before packaging the application. In the next section, we'll look at a few commonly used adapters and how they each produce builds specific to the intended environment.

Adapting the app

Now that we know how to build our application, we can explore some of the adapters that transform it for specified environments. For the entire time we've worked on our project, we've been using the @ sveltejs/adapter-auto package. So far, we haven't run into any issues, but if we want to build and deploy our application to a real production environment, we'll need to get more specific. While adapter-auto is great, it doesn't accept any configuration options and only works with Cloudflare Pages, Vercel, Netlify, and Azure Static Web Apps. If we wanted to host our application on a Node. js server or elsewhere, we would need to use a different adapter. Let's explore a few of the different options available in the following section. The adapters we'll look at are as follows:

- adapter-node
- adapter-cloudflare
- adapter-static

This list is not comprehensive, as the SvelteKit project supports many more environments. Meanwhile, the SvelteKit community continues creating and releasing adapters for a variety of platforms. Be sure to check the Svelte community resources before building your own adapter.

adapter-node

To begin, we'll start with adapter-node, as most web developers have at least some familiarity with Node.js environments. This adapter can be installed by running the following command:

```
npm install -D @sveltejs/adapter-node
```

Once installed, we can add it to our project by importing it into our svelte.config.js and specifying the adapter accordingly:

svelte.config.js

```
import adapter from '@sveltejs/adapter-node';
const config = {
    kit: {
        adapter: adapter(),
        alias: {
            db: '/src/db.js',
            img: '/src/lib/images'
        }
    },
};
export default config;
```

As before, this configuration only differs in that it imports `adapter-node` instead of `adapter-auto`.

Once the adapters have been switched out, we can build the application for a Node.js environment by running `npm run build` in the terminal. By default, this adapter will output the built application to the `build/` directory.

So far in this project, we've only included one dependency, and that was `bcrypt`. If we hadn't included that dependency, we wouldn't even need to do this next step. But because it seems rare to find a project that's not using other dependencies, we'd better cover it. To ensure our Node.js production environment has access to all the required dependencies, we'll need to install them. We do this by copying `package.json` and `package-lock.json` to the `build/` directory. To ensure our build works successfully, we'll simulate an automated deployment. We can do this by copying the entire `build/` directory (which now also includes `package.json` and `package-lock.json`) to another location on our machine. Once done, we can use npm's clean install command in the same directory to download the required production dependencies. This is the recommended installation method for automated deployments and continuous integration environments. We don't need development dependencies, as SvelteKit is now bundled into pure JS so the command looks like this:

```
npm ci --omit dev
```

Running this command in the same directory as our build will download the dependencies required.

We can then launch the application with the following command:

```
ORIGIN=http://0.0.0.0:3000 node build
```

In this instance, `build` is the name of the directory we would like Node.js to target. We've also specified the `ORIGIN` environment variable so that `adapter-node` can correctly determine the URL of the application. Without this, SvelteKit would block any `POST` requests as a means of protection against **Cross-Site Request Forgery** (**CSRF**) attacks. After running the command, we'll see that the application is listening on `0.0.0.0:3000`. To change the IP address or listening port, we can set those environment variables before running `node build`. For instance, launching the application at `127.0.0.1:8000` would look like `HOST=127.0.0.1 PORT=8000 ORIGIN=http://127.0.0.1:8000 node build`.

To further customize your builds, this adapter provides the following options:

- `out` – A string specifying the directory the build should be output to. It defaults to `build` and should not have a / character at the end.

- `precompress` – A Boolean value that defaults to `false` and controls whether or not assets and prerendered pages should be compressed using `gzip` and `brotli`.

- `envPrefix` – A string value specifying a prefix applied to environment variables, which proves quite useful when your hosting provider doesn't provide you with access to the standard environment variables such as `HOST` or `PORT`. Setting this will allow you to create your own environment variables.

- `polyfill` – A Boolean value defaulting to `true` that allows you to specify whether or not your build should include polyfills that add functionality not available in older Node.js releases.

After everything we've just covered, you should be able to deploy your own SvelteKit application to just about any Node.js environment. And if the destination environment limits your control, you should be able to customize the build using various options. Because Node.js environments are so prevalent, it would have been a huge mistake to not explain some of the functionality behind `adapter-node` and how it can streamline your deployment process.

adapter-cloudflare

While `adapter-node` is great for when we're running Node.js applications, there are adapters that allow us to deploy without needing to manage, configure, or maintain a server. Platforms such as Vercel, Netlify, and Cloudflare all provide these services and empower developers to ship their code faster than ever before. For demonstration purposes, let's look at how easy it is to deploy to Cloudflare Pages.

To begin, we'll install the adapter just like we have done with other packages:

```
npm i -D @sveltejs/adapter-cloudflare
```

Once done, we can change our `svelte.config.js` to reflect the new adapter. Again, we simply need to import the new adapter:

svelte.config.js

```
import adapter from '@sveltejs/adapter-cloudflare';
const config = {
    kit: {
        adapter: adapter(),
    }
};
export default config;
```

Before delving too deep, it's important to note that the application we have built thus far **will not deploy to Cloudflare** in its current state. Attempting to do so will result in many errors. In fact, you can see the errors for yourself by attempting to build the application using the Cloudflare adapter we just installed. The reason for this is quite simple. Cloudflare Workers and Pages do not run Node.js, which is required by one of our dependencies. While they are built off V8, which is the same engine that powers Node.js and Chromium-based browsers, they do not implement all of the APIs found in Node.js or those browsers. Instead, they exist as separate applications in their own right. And because we included the bcrypt package earlier, our application will fail to build as bcrypt makes extensive use of Node.js APIs. To successfully build and deploy the application, we will need to make a couple of changes.

If you'd prefer not to make these changes in your application, you can create a fork of this book's code repository found under the *Technical requirements* section listed at the beginning of each chapter. In that repository, there is a branch labeled cloudflare that has all of the necessary changes. When forking the repository, be sure to **deselect the box** that says **Copy the main branch only** as you will need the cloudflare branch. As for the necessary changes, let's take a brief detour and examine them now:

1. Uninstall bcrypt with the npm uninstall bcrypt command.

2. Remove references to bcrypt in src/routes/(app)/login/+page.server.js, as shown in the following code snippet.

3. Change src/lib/users.json passwords to plaintext values:

src/routes/(app)/login/+page.server.js

```
import users from '$lib/users.json';
export const actions = {
  login: async ({request, cookies}) => {
    const form = await request.formData();
    const exists = users.filter(user => user.username === form.
get('username'));
    const auth = exists.filter(user => user.password === form.
get('password'));

    if(!exists.length || !auth.length) {
      return {msg: 'Invalid login!'};
    }
    cookies.set('identity', auth[0].identity, {path: '/'});
    return {msg: 'success!'}
  }
}
```

This new version of +page.server.js simply removes references to the bcrypt package and instead compares the text supplied in the password field to the plain text values in the src/lib/users.json file. **It cannot be stressed how terrible this is from a security standpoint and I am trusting you to never do this outside of this particular demonstration**.

Now that we have removed all dependencies that require Node.js, we can proceed with our deployment to Cloudflare. Firstly, we should log in to a Cloudflare account, navigate to **Workers and Pages**, and click create application. From there, we can connect to a GitHub or GitLab account, and select a repository to connect with our Pages project. Cloudflare provides a few methods for moving your project to their platform, but we'll only cover how to do so by connecting with a Git repository. Once a repository is selected, we then provide a project name, which defaults to the repository name, and select a branch to deploy from. If you are deploying from a fork of this book's repository, you should specify `cloudflare` here. Typically, this would be the `main` branch.

From there, we can set up a few options. Cloudflare makes this next step a breeze by asking whether we're using a framework, which we are. Selecting **SvelteKit** from the **Framework preset** dropdown will auto-populate the **Build command** and **Build output directory** fields with the appropriate values. See *Figure 8.1* for more information:

Build settings 🗐 Configuring builds

If your project uses a static site generator or build tool, set the build instructions for Cloudflare.

Framework preset

> ⊗ SvelteKit   ▾

Select a framework to prefill recommended settings.

Build command ⓘ

> npm run build

e.g. npm run build

Build output directory ⓘ

> / .svelte-kit/cloudflare

e.g. dist

∨ Root directory (advanced)

Path

> / full_project

Your project's root directory, where Cloudflare runs the **build command**. If your site is not in a subdirectory, leave this path value empty.

∨ Environment variables (advanced)

Add variables to be used during build time for Production and Preview environments. Variables for each environment can be changed separately later.

Variable name   **Value**

> NODE_VERSION   =   18   ✕

＋ Add variable

Figure 8.1 – Cloudflare Pages project settings

Because the source code for the project we're attempting to deploy from is in a subdirectory of the Git repository, we'll have to specify that directory in the **Path** field. We then also need to specify `NODE_VERSION` in the **Environment variables** section. Though SvelteKit only requires Node.js 16.14 or higher, we've specified version 18 as that is the current latest Long-Term Support version of SvelteKit as well as the version used throughout the development of this book. Once everything has been filled out appropriately, you can save and deploy the project!

Cloudflare will then check out your code and attempt to build it. If everything is successful, you'll be provided with a URL pointing to your application. For reference, a version of the application we've created thus far is live at `https://sveltekit-up-and-running.pages.dev/`. Deploying an update to an application is as simple as pushing code to the appropriate branch in the project repository.

As you can see, deploying a SvelteKit application can be almost effortless once set up on serverless platforms such as Cloudflare Pages. The Vercel and Netlify adapters have similar processes, which you are encouraged to explore at your leisure. While our particular project ran into a slight issue with an included dependency requiring Node.js, this example hopefully demonstrated how using the right adapter can simplify deployments.

adapter-static

While we only ran into one minor problem with our previous adapter, we'll most certainly run into problems with `adapter-static`. The reason for that is that this adapter is intended to only be used on platforms that can host static content – that is, platforms where no server backend logic exists. If you have a host that can serve static HTML, CSS, and JS, you can host an entire SvelteKit application there using this adapter. A common example is GitHub pages, but Cloudflare and many others also support this method. Hosting static applications has the added benefit of increased speed since no server backend exists to communicate with.

Since we won't be able to get `adapter-static` working with our project, we won't attempt to install it on our existing project. But it is still an adapter worth discussing. Just like other adapters, it is easily installed via this command:

```
npm install -D @sveltejs/adapter-static
```

And again, it can then be imported in `svelte.config.js`. This adapter varies from the others in that it prerenders the entire application. It is able to do this because we will insert `export let prerender = true;` at the lowest level layout of our application. In each case, this will be `src/routes/+layout.js`.

To customize the builds produced with this adapter, we're provided with a few options. These options are passed to the adapter in `svelte.config.js`:

- `pages` – A string value defaulting to `build` that determines where prerendered pages will be output to.

- `assets` – A string value defaulting to the value provided to `pages` that determines where static assets should be output to.

- `fallback` – A string value specifying a fallback file to use when SSR has been disabled sitewide. Disabling SSR application-wide enables **Single-Page App (SPA)** mode. Typically, this is `index.html`, `200.html`, or `404.html`.

- `precompress` – A Boolean value that determines whether files should be compressed using `brotli` and `gzip` compression algorithms.

- `strict` – A Boolean value that prevents the application from building if certain endpoints will not exist when prerendered. It can be useful to disable if your application makes use of pages that exist only in specific circumstances.

If you're interested in trying `adapter-static` for yourself, consider creating a new SvelteKit application using the `skeleton` template. You can try with the *Demo App*, but will run into issues with server routes unable to be prerendered. These can be removed to get it working, but if your goal is to simply see how the static adapter works, it will likely be easier to deploy from the `skeleton` template. Again, the steps for building a static application are fairly straightforward:

1. Install the adapter with `npm install -D @sveltejs/adapter-static`.

2. Import the adapter in `svelte.config.js`.

3. Ensure the application is entirely prerenderable by adding `export let prerender = true;` in `src/routes/+layout.js`.

4. Run the `npm run build` command!

Once your application has been built, you can simply copy it to anywhere that can serve static files. Of course, certain hosts may have their own requirements so be sure to read their documentation as well.

A great way to learn about SvelteKit is by working with it. If you don't already have a personal website, consider creating one using the SvelteKit static adapter. Not only does it not require a database or backend but it can also be deployed to almost any hosting provider. If you're wondering where to start, Josh Collinsworth created a fantastic project using the static adapter. It enables users to add blog posts using Markdown while still existing as a static site. This means that hosting can be done for free on platforms such as GitHub Pages. You can find a link to Josh's project in the *Resources* section at the end of this chapter. While our project and many others cannot make use of `adapter-static` as they are not prerenderable, the value that this particular adapter provides for generating static sites is clear.

Summary

Having covered how the SvelteKit build process works, we then observed how we can preview our builds locally. We also looked at how page options can affect our builds. We took what we learned about the build process and saw how we can tailor our application to various platforms by selecting the right adapter. The application we've built so far is best suited to Node.js environments but we've also seen how simple it is to deploy to Cloudflare Pages and platforms such as Netlify or Vercel. By using the correct adapter and development strategies, we can even turn our application into a static website. Now that you've seen how to prepare your application for different production environments, you can go forth and release your SvelteKit applications into the wild.

In the next chapter, we'll learn how we can manipulate requests across our entire application through the use of hooks. We'll also address how we can utilize these hooks to assist in managing errors. Because no application is perfect, we'll address how SvelteKit lets us customize the user experience when issues do arise.

Resources

- *Svelte Society* – A central resource that provides many community-maintained Svelte-related projects including adapters: `https://sveltesociety.dev/`
- *How Cloudflare Workers Work*: `https://developers.cloudflare.com/workers/learning/how-workers-works`
- *SvelteKit Blog Starter* by Josh Collinsworth: `https://github.com/josh-collinsworth/sveltekit-blog-starter`

9

Hooks and Error Handling

While it can be incredibly useful to make API requests from any page, imagine the nuisance of attempting to authenticate a user for an external API on *every* page. It may be possible to create a custom helper that adds specific headers or cookies to every single request to assist with this. Fortunately for us, SvelteKit provides methods to manipulate Request and Response objects across the entirety of a framework. It does so with what are called **hooks**. These hooks can be incredibly powerful to manage data that flows in and out of our application. They can also be helpful for managing errors. Since our previous encounters with error handling have been so brief, we'll examine error handling a little closer after covering hooks.

In this chapter, we will cover the following topics:

- Using Hooks
- Error Handling

As a practical example, we'll build a simple interface allowing us to *star* the official SvelteKit repository on GitHub. You'll have to authenticate your personal account, but if you don't have an account on GitHub, fear not, as the concepts will be easy enough to follow along with. By the end of the exercise, we'll have covered the hooks available to use within SvelteKit, as well as how they can be leveraged to assist in managing errors.

Technical requirements

The complete code for this chapter is available on GitHub at: `https://github.com/PacktPublishing/SvelteKit-Up-and-Running/tree/main/chapters/chapter09`.

An account on GitHub is necessary to build the example: `https://github.com/signup`.

Using Hooks

Unlike other JS frameworks that shall not be named, SvelteKit keeps the list of hooks to remember short and simple. At the time of writing, there are only two types of hooks – **server hooks** and **shared hooks**. As we have come to expect from names, they work similarly to how `+page.server.js` runs only on the server and `+page.js` runs on either the server or the client. Both server and shared hooks are placed in the `src/` directory, either in `src/hooks.server.js` or `src/hooks.client.js`, depending on which environment we intend to run the hook on. We'll break this section down into the following subsections:

- Server hooks
- Shared hooks

By the end of this section, you'll be able to modify all incoming and outgoing requests to your SvelteKit applications.

Server hooks

The hooks that can only be run on the server are `handleFetch()` and `handle()`. As we would expect, `handleFetch()` has the ability to manipulate requests made by SvelteKit's included `fetch()` method, which can be called within `load()` or through actions. The other hook, `handle()`; can manipulate data as SvelteKit's router receives requests. One way to think of this is that `handleFetch()` manipulates the data *leaving* an app and `handle()` manipulates data *coming into* it. As server hooks, both can be added to `src/hooks.server.js`.

To begin this chapter's example to demonstrate how useful hooks can be, let's set up a few things. Firstly, we'll need a way to authenticate our personal account with GitHub. The manner in which we will achieve this is by sending a **personal access token** to the appropriate GitHub API endpoints. Once generated, this token can be added to the HTTP request headers. It's very important to treat tokens just as we treat passwords, so we'll import this token securely through environment variables, which will be discussed further in a later chapter.

To generate your token, visit `https://github.com` and sign in. You can then navigate to your profile settings by clicking your profile image in the top-right corner and selecting **Settings**. From there, scroll to the very bottom of the settings navigation pane and click **Developer Settings**. We'll then locate **Personal access tokens** and generate a *classic token*. Give the token a name, such as `SvelteKit star repo`, an expiration date, and the full *repo* scope. Once done, click **Generate Token** and copy the value provided.

We can then open our SvelteKit project and, in the root folder of the project, create a `.env` file. In this file, we'll add our token, like so:

.env

```
GITHUB=YOUR_GITHUB_TOKEN_HERE
```

You can then save and close the file. We'll go into more details on how how to manage secrets in a later chapter, but for now, just know that we've given our token a name using which we can import it into our code.

Next, let's create a new route and add it to `Nav.svelte`:

src/lib/Nav.svelte

```
<nav>
  <ul>
    <li><a href='/'>Home</a></li>
    ...
    <li><a href='/github'>GitHub</a></li>
  </ul>
</nav>
```

Again, this is a simple addition where we add markup for a link to our ever-growing list of links. Once we have added the markup for our new route to the navigation, we'll create the appropriate `+page.svelte` file to render the route. This page will consist of a simple form, with buttons allowing us to *star* and *unstar* the SvelteKit repository on GitHub, as well as some text showing just how many stars the repository currently has:

src/routes/(app)/github/+page.svelte

```
<script>
  import { enhance } from '$app/forms';
  import { invalidate } from '$app/navigation';
  export let data;
  export let form;
  const reload = () => {
    invalidate('https://api.github.com/repos/');
  };
</script>
{#if form && form.message }
  {form.status}
  {form.message}
{/if}
```

```
<p>
  Stargazers on the official SvelteKit repo: {data.repo.stargazers_
count}
</p>
<form method='POST' use:enhance>
  <button formaction='?/star' on:click={reload}>Star</button>
  <button formaction='?/unstar' on:click={reload}>Unstar</button>
</form>
```

There is quite a lot going on here, but it's nothing we haven't seen yet. Starting at the end of the file, we can see that this page contains a `<form>` element consisting of two buttons. One button calls to the `/github?/star` action and the other to the `/github?/unstar` action. The form uses the `enhance` module, meaning requests are made in the background and do not trigger a page reload. Each button inside the form calls the function expression assigned to the constant `reload`. That anonymous function utilizes the `invalidate` module, which then forces any `load()` functions with `fetch()` methods calling the specified URL to be rerun. This is helpful, as the paragraph tag showing how many stars the repository has will then be updated accordingly. The final portion of code to make note of is the Svelte `{#if}` directive, which will alert us to the status of the request.

Once we have saved `+page.svelte`, we'll need to move on to our `+page.server.js`, as it will contain the bulk of our logic. Importantly, it won't contain any of the code related to authentication, as all of that will reside in the hook:

src/routes/(app)/github/+page.server.js

```
const star_url = 'https://api.github.com/user/starred/sveltejs/kit';
export function load({ fetch }) {
  const repo = fetch( 'https://api.github.com/repos/sveltejs/kit' )
    .then( response => response.json() );
  return { repo };
}
export const actions = {
  star: async({ fetch }) => {
    const response = fetch(star_url, {
      method: 'PUT',
      headers: {
        'Content-Length': '0',
      }
    })
```

```
    .then(response => {
      const status = response.status;
      return {
        status: status,
        message: (status === 204 ? 'Success!' : 'Error')
      }
    });
    return response;
  },
  unstar: async({ fetch }) => {
    const response = fetch(star_url, {
      method: 'DELETE'
    })
    .then(response => {
      const status = response.status;
      return {
        status: status,
        message: (status === 204 ? 'Success!' : 'Error')
      }
    });
    return response;
  },
}
```

There is a lot going on here, but again, it's nothing we haven't seen before. The very first line declares a constant `star_url` that can be referenced in our `fetch()` requests later on. This is the endpoint we will reach out to alert GitHub that we want to *star* or *unstar* the repository. The very next chunk of code creates a familiar `load()` function. This endpoint does not actually require authentication and will return general information about the specified repository.

From there, we can examine the two actions we've created – *star* and *unstar*. Both of these destructure the **RequestEvent** object by retrieving the `fetch()` method bundled with SvelteKit. Both then use `fetch()` to make a request to the `star_url` endpoint but differ in the type of HTTP method they utilize, as per the GitHub API specifications. We've also added an extra header to the *star* request, as the official GitHub API documentation dictates that `Content-Body` should be set to 0 for this particular request. Both actions then return an object consisting of the request status and a message alerting us as to whether the request went through successfully, or whether an error was received.

At this point, we could navigate to `http://localhost/github` in our browser and view the number of stars on the official SvelteKit repository. However, attempting to star it will result in an error, as we won't have the appropriate permissions with the GitHub API. To authenticate, we'll need to provide our access token in the headers of our network requests. While we could do this in the `+page.server.js` file inside each of the actions, it would quickly become a hassle if we decided to build more routes that also required authentication with GitHub. For instance, what if we wanted to build functionality allowing us to read and react to comments on issues? Instead, we can use `handleFetch()` to catch all outgoing `fetch()` requests before they leave our application and authenticate in a single location. To do so, we'll need to create `src/hooks.server.js`:

src/hooks.server.js

```
import { GITHUB } from '$env/static/private';
export async function handleFetch( { request, fetch  } ) {
  if (request.url.startsWith('https://api.github.com/')) {
    request.headers.set('Accept', 'application/vnd.github+json');
    request.headers.set('Authorization', 'Bearer ' + GITHUB);
    request.headers.set('X-GitHub-Api-Version', '2022-11-28');
  }
  return fetch(request);
}
```

We begin by importing the personal access token we created earlier. Again, we'll examine how this works in a later chapter, so for now, just acknowledge that we've imported the token saved to `.env`. We then create the function definition for `handleFetch()`. Fetch is an asynchronous API, so we need to specify that this function will also be `async`. We've then destructured the `RequestEvent` object to extract `request` and `fetch`. Within the hook, we check to see whether the requested URL is `https://api.github.com/`. If it is, we'll then set the necessary `Accept`, `Authorization`, and `X-GitHub-Api-Version` headers. While `Accept` and `X-GitHub-Api-Version` are simple predetermined strings, the `Authorization` header value is the concatenated string *bearer*, as well as the imported personal access token.

We can now open `http://localhost/github` in our browser and click the *star* button. Because we've used `invalidate()` on the GitHub API URL, we should then observe the count increasing by one. The developers of SvelteKit have certainly earned our star, but if you're uncomfortable with this simple act of charity, try clicking the *unstar* button and observing the change again.

It's important to note that `handleFetch()` will only hook into the `fetch()` function provided by SvelteKit and not a standard `fetch()`. This can be observed by removing the destructured `fetch` parameter from the *star* and *unstar* actions in `src/routes/(app)/github/+page.server.js`. Then, attempting to star the repository will return an *unauthorized* error from the GitHub API, as the `handleFetch()` hook is not called unless we use the `fetch()` method provided with SvelteKit. This can also be observed by removing the destructured `fetch` from the `load()` function in +page.server.js. Provided you have not exceeded GitHub's rate limits, the standard fetch() function will continue providing data because the endpoint called to does not require authentication. Because of this, it is strongly encouraged to use SvelteKit's fetch() whenever possible.

As we can see, being able to manipulate requests leaving our application is quite powerful, but what about the requests coming into our platform? For that, we need to leverage handle(). For this example, we'll demonstrate it by adding the handle() hook of src/hooks.server.js:

src/hooks.server.js

```
import { GITHUB } from '$env/static/private';
export async function handleFetch( { request, fetch  } ) {
  if (request.url.startsWith('https://api.github.com/')) {
    request.headers.set('Accept', 'application/vnd.github+json');
    request.headers.set('Authorization', 'Bearer ' + GITHUB);
    request.headers.set('X-GitHub-Api-Version', '2022-11-28');
  }
  return fetch(request);
}
export async function handle({ event, resolve }) {
  event.setHeaders({'X-NOT-FROM-GITHUB': 'our value'});
  const response = await resolve(event);
  response.headers.set('X-ANOTHER-HEADER', 'something else');
  return response;
}
```

In this version, we've added the handle() function definition to the end of the file. This function accepts a RequestEvent object as well as a resolve() function. In our version, we've added a custom header that will be added to all requests within our application. That header is X-NOT-FROM-GITHUB and will contain the value *our value*. Once the header has been added to the event object, we complete the request by passing the event to resolve() and returning the promise. We've also added another method to demonstrate how you might go about modifying the headers after the request is made with resolve(). These headers can be observed by opening the browser on any page within our application, opening **Developer Tools**, navigating to the **Network** tab, and refreshing the page. Opening the very first request will show our custom headers and values in **Response Headers**.

Of course, we're not limited to setting only headers. Headers were chosen simply for demonstration purposes. We can also set data that will be made available to us in load() and server pages by setting event.locals to the object of our choosing. We can even utilize event.cookies to modify cookie values. However, if we use SvelteKit's included fetch() method, those cookies will automatically be passed within the application, so long as it lives at a domain that has permission to access the cookies. One final note to make is that both handle() and handleFetch() will run either on render or during the prerendering process. This is particularly important to remember if you're attempting to generate a static site using adapter-static.

As we just demonstrated, server hooks can be a powerful tool to leverage when you need to customize request and response headers. While modifying header data is only one use case for them, the example we provided should highlight the many possible solutions they can address. Next, let's take a look at the hooks available to us on the client as well as the server.

Shared hooks

Having just covered the two hooks available in server environments, we now only have `handleError()` available to us in client environments. This hook is useful for capturing errors that weren't thrown through the use of SvelteKit's `error` module – that is, any critical application errors, or errors thrown using `throw new Error()`. It can be very useful to log application errors. It also allows us to control what users will see when they encounter a serious issue with an application. To demonstrate how a shared hook works, let's add it to both `src/hooks.server.js` and `src/hooks.client.js`. In this example, we'll log errors on the server to a file and errors on the client using `console.log()`:

src/hooks.client.js

```
export async function handleError({ error, event }) {
   console.log('client handled error' + error.message);
   console.log(event.url);
   return {message: 'Whoops, looks like you found an error! Sorry about that.'};
}
```

In this example, we use `console.log()` to show various messages within the browser console. It would be nice if `handleError()` ran for every unexpected error within the client; however, that is not the case, as it only runs if an error is encountered during a client-side `load()` or while rendering on the client. As such, we'll need to throw an error in another location to see it in action. To trigger this error, we'll make a minor change to `src/routes/(site)/fetch/+page.js`:

src/routes/(site)/fetch/+page.js

```
import { browser } from '$app/environment';
const key = 'DEMO_KEY'; // your API key here
export const prerender = true;
export function load() {
  if(browser) {
    throw new Error('in the browser');
  }
  const pic = fetch(`https://api.nasa.gov/planetary/apod?api_
key=${key}`)
    .then(response => {
      console.log('got response');
```

```
      return response.json();
   });
  return {pic};
}
```

The first change we make is importing the `browser` module from `$app/environment`. Once done, we check that the code being run is in the browser and then throw an error, leaving the rest of the code alone. When we navigate to the `/fetch` route in our application, we'll see the messages output from `src/hooks.client.js`. With this hook, we can ensure that no sensitive data is output to the client during client-side errors. We can also tailor the message in the returned error object accordingly.

To demonstrate `handleError()` on the server, we can write the error messages to a log file, which can be easily read at a later time by developers or a daemon installed on the server:

src/hooks.server.js

```
import { GITHUB } from '$env/static/private';
import fs from 'fs';
export async function handleFetch( { request, fetch } ) {
  if (request.url.startsWith('https://api.github.com/')) {
    request.headers.set('Accept', 'application/vnd.github+json');
    request.headers.set('Authorization', 'Bearer ' + GITHUB);
    request.headers.set('X-GitHub-Api-Version', '2022-11-28');
  }
  return fetch(request);
}
export async function handle({ event, resolve }) {
  event.setHeaders({'X-NOT-FROM-GITHUB': 'our value'});
  const response = await resolve(event);
  response.headers.set('another', 'custom value');
  return response;
}

function today() {
  const current = new Date();
  return current.getDate() + "-" +
         current.getDay() + "-" +
         current.getFullYear() + " " +
         current.getHours() + ":" +
         current.getMinutes() + ":" +
         current.getSeconds();
}
export async function handleError({ error, event }) {
```

```
  const log = today() + ' ' + error.message + ' @ ' + event.request.
url;
  fs.appendFile('./app.log', log + '\n', (err) => {
    if(err) {
      console.log(err);
    }
  });
  return {
    error: error.message
  };
}
```

The first change in this example to note is that we've imported the `fs` module. This is a Node-specific module for accessing the filesystem. This is worth noting, as including it will prevent us from building our application for another environment. The next change to note is that we've added the `today()` function, which returns the current date and time as a string. Ideally, this function would live in a `utilities` folder, likely located in `src/lib/`, but for this demonstration, we can include it here. We've also added `handleError()` to the end of the file. It accepts an `error` object as well as an `event` object. We then concatenate the output from the `today()` function with the error message, as well as information about where the error occurred. This is all then written to our log file using `fs.appendFile()`. If an error is encountered while writing to the file, we'll output it to the console. Finally, we return an object containing the error message.

To trigger `handleError()`, we can throw an error in one of our actions or `load()`. The precise location isn't particularly important, but we can see our logging in action by adding `throw new Error('our custom error');` to `+page.server.js`. In fact, try throwing an error from various `load()` functions or actions we've created so far. You can even experiment with the data provided from the request. For example, it might be helpful to log various headers, such as the client User-Agent, as this information can be helpful when troubleshooting browser compatibility. Once you have thrown a few errors, open `app.log` in the root of the project directory and observe the output. This simple logging mechanism can be tailored to a project's needs.

By leveraging `handleError()`, we can effortlessly bootstrap our own logging mechanism. We can also customize messages shown during errors on client-side rendering or `load()`, which is especially helpful if our application is a single-page app. Of course, `handleError()` is very helpful, but it's only helpful for unexpected errors. How should we manage errors that we fully expect?

Error Handling

Oftentimes, pesky users attempt to access resources they're not supposed to access. Or maybe they're just users being users and not paying attention to where they're clicking. In any case, we've all met at least one user like this. As developers, it is in our best interest to ensure our code gives those users meaningful messages when they inevitably encounter an error. For the sake of our sanity and future selves, we should discuss errors in SvelteKit.

All of the errors we just created with `handleError()` are considered *unexpected errors*. That is because we did not use SvelteKit's error module. Errors created using this module are considered *expected errors*. By importing the module, we can send custom status codes and error messages to SvelteKit, which can then be captured and used by `+error.svelte` components. This gives us even greater control over how our messaging displays to users.

In *Chapter 4*, we briefly examined how the routing mechanism will interact with the closest `+error.svelte` template available. However, we didn't really discuss the `error` module or how to use it. Firstly, it needs to be imported from `@sveltejs/kit`. Once imported, we can then throw the error with `throw error()` and pass the function two arguments. The first argument is an integer representing the HTTP status code classifying the error. For instance, a `401` code represents a *client unauthorized* error. The second argument passed to `error()` is an object containing a message property, with the message we would like conveyed.

To see an example, let's make some modifications to our previous code:

src/routes/(app)/github/+page.server.js

```javascript
import { error } from '@sveltejs/kit';
const star_url= 'https://api.github.com/user/starred/sveltejs/kit';

export function load({ fetch }) {
  throw error(401, {
    message: 'You don\'t have permission to see this!',
    id: crypto.randomUUID()
  });
  const repo = fetch( 'https://api.github.com/repos/sveltejs/kit' )
    .then( response => response.json() );
  return { repo };
}
export const actions = {
    // omitted for brevity
}
```

In this example, we've imported the `error` module from `@sveltejs/kit`. Within the `load()` function, we then immediately throw an error using the module. For our error, we supply the `401` status code and an object with `message` properties, as well as a custom error `id`. Again, this can be helpful for reporting and logging errors because we can customize the error object with whatever information we'd like to provide. If we prefer not to create a whole object, we can instead provide a string with the error message or even just the HTTP status code! We'll leave the rest of the code in this file unchanged.

Instead of building a traditional `try catch` statement around the error, we'll let SvelteKit handle the catching by providing a customized `+error.svelte` component:

src/routes/(app)/github/+error.server.js

```
<script>
  import { page } from '$app/stores';
</script>
{$page.error.message}
{#if $page.error.id}
  <p>
    Error ID: {$page.error.id}
  </p>
{/if}
```

To show our error messages, we'll have to leverage the data within the Svelte store `page`. This store is imported from `$app/stores`, and the data within it can be accessed by prefacing the store name with a `$` symbol. The `page` store contains various properties and data pertaining to the accessed page. We then show the provided error message, followed by a Svelte `{#if}` directive to show the error ID, provided it exists.

We can then navigate to `http://localhost/github` and view our new error message, as well as an error ID number. To play around with this example and learn a little more about error handling, try moving `src/routes/(app)/github/+error.svelte` to `src/routes/(app)/+error.svelte`. What happens if you move it all the way up to `src/routes/+error.svelte`? You should try this in your own project, but in short, Svelte's routing mechanism is robust enough to take the error to the nearest `+error.svelte` component it finds.

Having explored error handling, you should now be able to show your application users pertinent information related to the error they've stumbled across. Doing so in an informative way should minimize the time spent triaging support tickets.

Summary

Having explored the various hooks available in SvelteKit as well as error handling, we've covered a lot. We first saw how we can modify outgoing `fetch()` requests that leverage SvelteKit's included `fetch()` by changing familiar `RequestEvent` objects in the `handleFetch()` hook. We also saw how we can adjust data flowing into our application via `handle()`. Then, we explored the `handleError()` shared hook and how it can be utilized to build a rich logging mechanism or incorporated with another service. Finally, we returned to look at how we can manage expected errors with SvelteKit's error routing devices, which allow us to customize the look and feel through custom Svelte components.

Now that we have a firm grasp on how to manage errors, we'll move on to the next chapter to assess how we can best manage static assets.

Resources

- GitHub API documentation: `https://docs.github.com/en/rest`

10
Managing Static Assets

When it comes to managing static assets, SvelteKit has little to do with the process. In fact, the entire process is handed over to the bundling tool Vite. By leveraging Vite for the management of static assets, we as developers don't have to learn yet another framework-specific strategy. Instead, we can lean on Vite's highly performant bundling and build processes. Because Vite automatically manages imported assets, we don't have to worry about hashing files for caches. In this chapter, we'll look at how we can leverage Vite to manage static assets such as images, fonts, audio, video, and CSS files. Once we examine *how* this is done, we'll discuss some of the finer points surrounding static assets.

This chapter will be divided into the following sections:

- Importing Assets
- Additional Information

By the time we're done, we'll have a firm grasp of the best practices to use when including files that can be served *as is* within SvelteKit applications.

Technical requirements

The complete code for this chapter is available on GitHub at: `https://github.com/PacktPublishing/SvelteKit-Up-and-Running/tree/main/chapters/chapter10`.

Importing Assets

If you have worked in web development for the past decade, then you'll remember a time when styles were written either inline or in a **Cascading Style Sheet** (**CSS**). These **CSS** files are helpful for creating a consistent look and feel for an application. Of course, their centralized nature comes with its own drawbacks. They often become large and difficult to navigate, which can lead to the inclusion of unused style rules. When precious milliseconds can mean the difference between converting a user or losing a sale, it's important not to ship unused assets to clients. Besides, if we're building a web application with SvelteKit, we really should use the Svelte approach and keep styles isolated within each component. But there are times when it's useful to keep a style sheet that applies some global styles. For instance, imagine having to apply a specific style to each and every paragraph element. Incorporating the same simple style rule into every component across the application could lead to repetitive code. There may even be instances where we forget to include a rule, leading to inconsistent styles across the app. And while projects such as **Tailwind CSS** or **Bootstrap** are wonderful, they may not be appropriate for every project, which is why we're going to cover how to include a global style sheet in our SvelteKit application.

To begin, we'll need some styles. Keep in mind that these styles will apply to the entirety of the application. Normally, when creating styles within Svelte components, those styles are isolated to that specific component, meaning they are not applied to parent or child components. Many modern browsers apply their own default styles to HTML elements, and so, to unify the experience of an application, it's common practice to create a `reset.css` file. This file ensures the experience is consistent across different browsers by resetting the styles applied by browsers of common elements to something predictable. For our example, we'll use a slightly modified version of the concise yet thorough **Custom CSS Reset** by *Josh W. Comeau*. See the resources at the end of this chapter for links to the article explaining exactly how it works:

src/reset.css

```
/* https://www.joshwcomeau.com/css/custom-css-reset/ */
*, *::before, *::after {
  box-sizing: border-box;
}
* {
  margin: 0;
}
html, body {
  height: 100%;
  font-family: sans-serif;
}
body {
  line-height: 1.5;
  -webkit-font-smoothing: antialiased;
}
```

```
img, picture, video, canvas, svg {
  display: block;
  max-width: 100%;
}
input, button, textarea, select {
  font: inherit;
}
p, h1, h2, h3, h4, h5, h6 {
  overflow-wrap: break-word;
}
```

In essence, the rules of this CSS file are setting more sane and predictable default styles for various HTML elements. For instance, `box-sizing` is set to `border-box`, which applies to all elements, as well as the `::before` and `::after` pseudo-elements. This rule means that the padding of elements will be included when calculating that element's width. These CSS rules allow a consistent and reliable experience across browsers. Of course, we're free to make any additions to this CSS. To make our changes slightly more noticeable, we've also set `font-family: sans-serif;` on both the `html` and `body` elements.

To include this CSS in our application, we'll open `src/routes/+layout.svelte` and import it just as we would a JS module. If you remember back to *Chapter 2*, we used the same method to import an image path!

src/routes/+layout.svelte

```
<script>
  import '/src/reset.css';
  import Nav from '$lib/Nav.svelte';
  import Notify from '$lib/Notify.svelte';
  export let data;
</script>
...
```

Noticeably, the only change we need to make in this file is the very first line where we import `reset.css`. The remaining code has been omitted from the file for the sake of brevity. After importing the CSS file, notice that our styles are immediately applied. We don't need to create `<link>` or `<style>` tags as Vite recognizes the style sheet for what it is and automatically applies it for us. Conveniently, the file import path can be relative or absolute as Vite makes no distinction between the two.

To highlight the benefits of importing a stylesheet with this method, let's compare it with another method for including global style sheets. This method was applied to pre-1.0 releases of SvelteKit and worked by manually adding a `<link>` tag to the `<head>` section of `src/app.html`. It then referenced a file within the `static/` directory using the `%sveltekit.assets%` placeholder. This method is ill-advised but let's analyze it to consider its faults:

src/app.html

```
<!DOCTYPE html>
<html lang="en">
  <head>
    <meta charset="utf-8" />
    <link rel="icon" href="%sveltekit.assets%/favicon.png" />
    <meta name="viewport" content="width=device-width" />
    <link rel="stylesheet" href="%sveltekit.assets%/global.css" />
      %sveltekit.head%
  </head>
  <body data-sveltekit-preload-data="hover">
    <div style="display: contents">%sveltekit.body%</div>
  </body>
</html>
```

As we can see, this method includes the `static/global.css` file inside the head tag of `src/app.html`, the application entry point. The `app.html` file works as scaffolding for the rest of the application to build off of, so it stands to reason that we could include any extraneous scripts or external assets here, just as the favicon is included. This method relies on the `%sveltekit.assets%` placeholder to include the CSS file from the `static/` directory. However, this method fails to consider Vite's HMR features. Whenever changes are made to `static/global.css`, the entire development server will need to be restarted to reflect those changes as Vite does not process any of the files included in the static assets. Also consider the common scenario of applying minification to `.css` and preprocessing to `.scss`, `.sass`, or `.less` files. In each of these instances, we would need Vite to take a more hands-on approach than it does for files included from SvelteKit's `static/` directory. And because Vite can manage cached files by appending hashes to the filenames of static assets, it is clear that importing files just as we would import a JS module is in our best interest.

In *Chapter 2*, we saw how we could import an image URL. We've now also seen how Vite allows us to import a global CSS file directly into our Svelte components. Now that we've shown how to best utilize static assets dynamically with our applications, let's discuss some more of the details surrounding this process.

Additional Information

We now know *how* we can import static files, but there are a few details to keep in mind when doing so. Here's a breakdown of the various items we still need to cover:

- Images versus Styles
- Customizing Imports
- File Paths
- SvelteKit Configuration Options
- Vite Configuration Options

Now let's go over some important information about what went on behind the scenes with each of our imports.

Images versus Styles

When we imported an image in *Chapter 2*, we received the URL, which we then referenced in the `src` attribute of an `<img>` tag. When we imported the CSS file, we only needed to import it to apply the styles. This is because Vite is pre-configured to automatically inject the styles from CSS files into the component performing the import. Hence why the import was performed in the root `+layout.svelte` file. Vite also supports CSS `@import` and `url()` statements as well as CSS modules. CSS modules can be useful for importing style rules as objects within code whereas `@import` and `url()` allow developers to build a central CSS file that can reference smaller CSS files located elsewhere. When importing a CSS file, no other action needs to be taken other than the import. When importing other media such as fonts, audio, or video files, we'll need to set the imported asset URL as the `src` attribute on the appropriate HTML element.

Customizing Imports

When importing static assets from Vite, we can customize how they are imported by appending the appropriate suffix to the file import names. For instance, to import a file as a string, we can append `?raw` to the filename. As expected, this will give us the raw content of the imported file. For the `reset.css` example shown earlier, it could be included via `import reset from '/src/reset.css?raw';` where the reset variable contains the content from `reset.css`. We would then need to find a way to include that content inside of `<style>` tags. In a similar fashion, if we want to import a file as a URL that is not found in the standard media types, we can append `?url` to the file import statement. This can be helpful for including files served from a **Content Delivery Network (CDN)**. We can even import scripts as web workers by appending `?worker` to the filename!

File Paths

When running Vite's development server, we can observe the network requests in our browser's developer tools and notice that imported files are served from their location within the project source code. For example, the image from *Chapter 2* is located at `src/lib/images/demo.svg` and is also served from that very same location. However, when we run `npm run build` followed by `npm run preview`, we'll observe that the path has changed. It is given the path `_app/immutable/assets/demo.dd76856a.svg`. This path is specific to the built SvelteKit application and, normally, we won't edit it after the application has been built. But take a moment to notice that a hash has been included in the filename. Should the file contents change, we'll notice the built asset will include a different hash appended to the file's name.

We can also take this moment to observe the included favicon file. We'll see that in both `dev` and `build/preview`, it is served from the domain root directory `/`. This is because it was located in the `static/` directory and Vite serves and builds the application so that any files located there will be served from the root level of the application.

SvelteKit Configuration Options

These options can be customized in `svelte.config.js`:

- `files.assets` – This option specifies the directory for which static assets will be stored. SvelteKit automatically sets this option to `static` and overrides the Vite sibling setting specified as `publicDir` (which defaults to `public`). Files that normally fit here are `robots.txt` or `favicon.ico` as they rarely change. To reference files located here in the source code, simply prefix the filename with `/`. For instance, we can show the default favicon by adding `<img src='/favicon.png' />` to any component.

- `paths.assets` – This option takes a string that specifies the absolute path from where application files are served. It defaults to an empty string.

- `paths.base` – This option also defaults to an empty string. If your application is being served from a sub-directory, you can specify the root-relative path here. Then, you may use the `base` module imported from `$app/paths` to modify hardcoded paths appropriately.

- `paths.relative` – This option accepts a Boolean value. When `true`, the values provided by `base` and `assets` from the `$app/paths` module will be relative to built assets. When `false`, those same values with be root-relative.

Vite Configuration Options

This option can be customized in a project's `vite.config.js`:

- `assetsInclude` – Many common media types are automatically handled by Vite but this option can be useful if a project needs to extend the default list to treat uncommon file types as assets. This option allows for the customization of allowable static asset file types. It can be a string, regular expression, or **picomatch** pattern.

We've just seen how we can customize the importing of static assets. If we need to force an asset to be imported as a URL, we know that we append ?url to the end of the imported file. We've also learned how CSS files are automatically injected into the component they are imported to. Along with a few configuration options, these details provide insight into how we can make the management of static assets stress-free in our SvelteKit applications.

Summary

When including images, CSS files, or other media types in SvelteKit applications, it is clear that we should leverage Vite to import the asset just as we would import a JS module. Doing so comes with the advantage of being simple but also allowing for optimized caches. It keeps our development experience smooth as Vite's HMR will automatically show changes in the browser. It's also flexible in that it allows for various media types to be imported either by URL or raw content.

Now that we know how to manage static assets, we should circle back to how we manage secrets. If you recall the previous chapter, we added a personal access token to the .env file, which allowed us to authenticate with the GitHub API. In the next chapter, we'll explore this further and cover the various modules that make managing secrets a breeze.

Resources

- Tailwind CSS – `https://tailwindcss.com/`
- Bootstrap – `https://getbootstrap.com/`
- Josh W. Comeau's Custom CSS Reset – `https://www.joshwcomeau.com/css/custom-css-reset/`
- Vite Configuration Options – `https://vitejs.dev/config/`
- CSS Modules – `https://github.com/css-modules/css-modules`
- picomatch – `https://github.com/micromatch/picomatch`

11

Modules and Secrets

While routing is certainly important to SvelteKit, there is far more to it than just that. Throughout this book, we've utilized multiple different SvelteKit modules. For instance, we've imported bindings from $app/forms, $app/environment, and $app/stores, to name a few. But we have yet to explore what these modules are or how they work. In this chapter, we'll give a brief overview of some of the modules we've seen previously as well as some we have not yet seen. We'll also cover some of the modules used for managing secrets and when to use which ones.

In this chapter, we'll examine the following:

- SvelteKit Module Summaries
- Keeping Secrets Safe

Having covered various modules, as well as examining our previous example of storing GitHub API secrets, we'll have a clear understanding of when best to harness the power of each individual module.

Technical requirements

The complete code for this chapter is available on GitHub at: `https://github.com/PacktPublishing/SvelteKit-Up-and-Running/tree/main/chapters/chapter11`.

SvelteKit Module Summaries

In previous chapters, we've used several different modules but only provided short explanations. While the analysis in this section will also be brief, it should provide a broad enough insight that prospective SvelteKit developers feel familiar with the workings of available modules. We have encountered a few listed here but there are some that we are yet to cover. For more in-depth explanations, see the resources at the end of this chapter.

$app/environment

To begin our analysis of modules, let's start with one that we have used relatively recently. In *Chapter 9*, while attempting to throw an error in the client, we used the $app/environment module and imported browser. As we've come to expect with SvelteKit naming conventions, all of the bindings exported from this module pertain to the application environment. This makes it trivial to identify the purpose of each of the bindings by their names. For instance, we saw that browser returns a Boolean value based on whether or not the environment it is being run in is the client. Likewise, building and dev will return Boolean values based on whether or not the code is being run during the build process or in our development environment, respectively. The final export from $app/environment is version. While version is still appropriately named, it's important to note that it doesn't refer to the version of SvelteKit. Rather, it refers to the version of the application build. The value of version is determined by the Unix timestamp at the time of building. SvelteKit uses this string value to check for a new version when client-side navigation encounters an error and defaults to standard navigation practices by making a full-page load.

$app/forms

When we utilized enhance from $app/forms in *Chapter 4*, we saw how it could *progressively enhance* our form submissions by sending data in the background instead of requiring our entire page to be reloaded when submitting the form. If the default behavior of enhance has not quite satisfied our needs, it can be customized. If we decide to change its default behavior and provide it with a custom callback function, applyAction can be used to update the data within the form property of our components. The final binding we can import from $app/forms is deserialize, which is a helpful function when deserializing response data from a form submission.

$app/navigation

As expected, $app/navigation provides tools pertaining to navigation. We previously used invalidateAll in *Chapter 5* and invalidate in *Chapter 9* from this module. In both of those instances, we did so to force load() to run again. Some other helpful bindings from this module are afterNavigate and beforeNavigate. Both of these bindings run callback functions at specific timings within the SvelteKit life cycle. With afterNavigate, the provided callback is executed once the current component has mounted and after the user has navigated to a new URL. The callback function for beforeNavigate is run just before navigating to a new URL.

Some other bindings available from this particular module include `disableScrollHandling`, `goto`, `preloadCode`, and `preloadData`. If we wanted to change how SvelteKit manages the browser window scrolling position, we could disable it entirely by calling `disableScrollHandling()`. The `goto()` function provides developers with the ability to navigate to another URL while also including options that allow for the management browser history, keeping focus applied to a particular element, and even triggering the rerun of `load()` functions. The `preloadCode()` function allows developers to import the code for a particular route before that route has been navigated to, while `preloadData()` will do the same as well as calling the route's `load()` function. The same behavior of `preloadData()` is found when `<a>` elements are given the `data-sveltekit-preload-data` attribute.

$app/paths

When we need to manipulate file paths or create links to routes for our application that reside in a sub-directory, we can rely on `$app/paths`. Both `assets` and `base` will return a string value that can be customized in `svelte.config.js` under `config.kit.paths`. If the application is being served from a subdirectory, we can prepend manually written routes with the `{base}` text to ensure our application serves the route from the correct directory and does not attempt to serve the route from the domain root directory. The value provided by `base` must always be a root-relative path that begins with a / but never ends with one. Conversely, `assets` will always be an absolute path to the application files.

$app/stores

The SvelteKit developers were kind enough to provide developers with a few readable stores that can supply us with helpful information. When importing from `$app/stores`, we'll have access to `navigating`, `page`, `updated`, and `getStores`. During navigation, `navigating` will be populated with an object consisting of metadata such as where the navigation event started, where it is going, and the type of navigation. The type can range from a form submission to a link click, or even a browser back-and-forward event. Once navigation has been completed, the value of this store will return to `null`. Meanwhile, `page` serves as a store that contains information related to the currently viewed page. We used it back in *Chapter 4* to display the current page's error message. The `updated` store will return a Boolean value after SvelteKit has checked whether or not a new version of the application has been detected. All of these stores can be retrieved by calling `getStores()` but doing so is not recommended and should only be done when the store subscription needs to be paused until after a component has mounted. Otherwise, all store values can be accessed by prefixing the store name with the $ symbol, which will automatically handle the subscription process.

$service-worker

When building a **PWA**, we will inevitably find ourselves configuring a service worker. For these cases, we're provided with the `$service-worker` module, which can only be used within a service worker. When importing bindings, we'll have access to `base`, `build`, `files`, `prerendered`, and `version`. Again, sane naming conventions come to our rescue and mostly explain the type of data returned from each of these bindings. We can receive a string value from `base`, which works similarly to the `base` from `$app/paths`. It will provide us with the base path to the application even if the application exists in a subdirectory. The array of strings from `build` will consist of URLs generated by Vite during the build process. Another array of strings, `files`, will provide details on static files or those included in `config.kit.files.assets`. For prerendered path names, we can retrieve the strings from the `prerendered` array. And finally, we can use `version` to determine the application version within our service worker code.

This list of modules is by no means comprehensive. Before leaning on them too heavily, it's recommended to read the official SvelteKit documentation listed at the end of this chapter. Now that we've examined some of these modules, let's move on to the modules that help us keep sensitive information safe.

Keeping secrets safe

When it comes to keeping secrets such as API keys or database credentials safe, SvelteKit has us covered. As we saw in *Chapter 9*, we can import `.env` secrets from `$env/static/private`. But this is not the only module that allows us to import environment variables. In this section, we'll examine more modules and how they all can help us import environment variables as well as secrets.

$env/static/private

Beginning with the module we've already used, `$env/static/private` is great for importing environment variables like those specified in `.env` files or those set when starting the runtime. For instance, if we were to start our application with the `API_KEY="" node index.js` command, the `API_KEY` variable would be available, just as `GITHUB` was available after we imported `$env/static/private` in *Chapter 9*. Any environment variables provided when starting the application will override the value of those provided in a `.env` file. The variables from this module are statically bundled within the application code at build time by Vite. This means less bundled code but also means that secrets will be included in the application build. We can confirm this by building the following commands:

```
npm run build
grep -r 'YOUR_API_KEY' .svelte-kit/
```

Substituting `YOUR_API_KEY` with your personal access token provided by GitHub will show the text and the file in our build where our API key has been injected. As such, we should be cautious not to commit builds to version control as doing so could then expose secrets. Fortunately for us, this module will only work with server-side code and will cause a build to fail if we attempt to import it into client-side code.

$env/static/public

We can consider `$env/static/public` a sibling to `$env/static/private`. The major difference is that this module will only import variables that begin with the value set in `config.kit.env.publicPrefix`. By default, this value is `PUBLIC_`. This allows us to keep our secrets all in the same `.env` file while allowing us to specify which are safe to expose to clients and which are not. For example, the following `.env` file would allow for `PUBLIC_GITHUB_USER` to be imported into client-side code but not `GITHUB_TOKEN`. Even though both values exist in the same file, we can rest assured knowing that SvelteKit won't tell our secrets to anyone other than the server we know we can trust:

.env

```
GITHUB_TOKEN=YOUR_GITHUB_PERSONAL_ACCESS_TOKEN
PUBLIC_GITHUB_USER=YOUR_USERNAME_HERE
```

$env/dynamic/private

Just as we cannot import `$env/static/private` into client-side code, we cannot import `$env/dynamic/private` into client-side code either. The difference between these two modules is that while the `$env/static` modules have access to `.env` files, `$env/dynamic` has access to the environment variables specified by the adapter. Think back to *Chapter 8* when we deployed our application to Cloudflare. When we did that, we specified the environment variable `NODE_VERSION`. Obtaining the Node version likely isn't very useful to us but using `$env/dynamic/private` allows us to access other secrets set in our Cloudflare Pages project settings. This can be helpful when working in a team as sharing secrets can be done on the platform rather than passing around `.env` files. When the platform the project will be deployed to has its own means of setting environment variables, it's very likely you'll be relying on `$env/dynamic` to access them.

$env/dynamic/public

By following the established pattern, this module should need little explanation. With `$env/dynamic/public`, we will only be able to import environment variables that begin with `PUBLIC_` or whatever value has been specified in `config.kit.env.publicPrefix`. This works in the same way as `$env/static/public`. Of course, it differs from `$env/static/public` because this is another dynamic module, which means it is specific to the configured environment adapter. For instance, if we were to add `PUBLIC_GITHUB_USER` to our Cloudflare Pages environment variables, we would then be able to access the value of that environment variable using this module.

Summary

There are a great many modules available within SvelteKit. Hopefully, this brief overview has given enough insight so that we know where to start with each of them. In the next chapter, we'll examine some best practices for enhancing accessibility, which can come with the added benefit of improving **Search Engine Optimization (SEO)**.

Resources

- SvelteKit Module Documentation – `https://kit.svelte.dev/docs/modules`

12
Enhancing Accessibility and Optimizing SEO

When it comes to building web applications, we cannot disregard how important it is to ensure the applications are accessible to all users. By empowering those who rely on assistive technologies such as screen readers, we can further the impact our applications have. Not only does making an application available to a wider audience bring in more users, but it can also affect **Search Engine Optimization (SEO)**. Therefore, it would be negligent to disregard how SvelteKit can help us make our applications accessible from the start.

To understand how we can best empower our users and how doing so can help boost our SEO, we should examine a few concepts. Firstly, we'll see how the built-in compile-time checks can improve the accessibility of our application with little configuration on our end. We'll also see how to best announce route changes, which can benefit tools such as screen readers. We'll then briefly cover a few more tips that can benefit accessibility and wrap up with some simple tips for improving SEO. We'll break it all apart into the following sections:

- Compile-time checks
- Announcing routes
- Accessibility enhancements
- SEO tips

Upon completing this chapter, we'll have covered the essentials for ensuring your SvelteKit applications are accessible to a wide audience. Following the best practices outlined here will have the added benefit of improving SEO rankings.

Technical requirements

The complete code for this chapter is available on GitHub at: https://github.com/PacktPublishing/SvelteKit-Up-and-Running/tree/main/chapters/chapter12

Compile-Time Checks

When we installed our SvelteKit project, it came with a few opinionated enhancements out of the box. Of those enhancements, the compile-time checks can be of particular use to warn us of elements that have been poorly formed or are missing attributes. Upon making the suggested changes, we'll notice that these warnings go away.

If you've paid attention to the recommendations from `eslint` or the output from builds, you may have noticed some warnings referring to `A11y`. This is the abbreviated term used for *Accessibility*. It refers to the *A*, the following 11 characters, and the *y*. In recognizing the importance of making applications accessible, the Svelte developers have opted to include sane behaviors by default as it contributes to a more open web. Before becoming frustrated with regular warnings, consider the convenience of having the application checked for a11y errors while not having to seek out our own solutions. Not only does building with a11y in mind help users but it also helps developers become better by recognizing which patterns are accessible and which are not.

If you've yet to see any of these issues, we can go back to one of our earliest examples and remove an `alt` attribute from an `<img>` element:

src/routes/+page.svelte

```
<script>
  import db from 'db';
  import url from 'img/demo.svg';
  let status = db.connection;
  let name = 'World';
</script>
<form>
  <label for="name" >What is your name?</label>
  <input type="text" class='name' bind:value={name} />
</form>
<h1>Hello, {name}!</h1>
<p>{status}</p>
<img src={url}>
// A11y: <img> element should have an alt attribute
```

In this example, the only change made is the removal of the `alt` attribute from the `<img>` tag at the very end. Most modern editors should alert you directly in the file, but if you're not seeing this warning, you can view it directly in the output from the build by running `npm run build` in your terminal. Upon observing the `build` output, we will be able to discern the exact location of the problem and view a recommended fix.

These warnings don't only apply to missing attributes on HTML elements either. We'll also be alerted if form labels are associated with a control, if certain media types have captions, if attributes are given improper values, and more warnings than can be reasonably listed here. For a full list, see the resources at the end of this chapter. As we can see, the compile-time a11y checks can be incredibly useful in helping developers deliver accessible applications to as many users as possible.

Following the advice of compile-time check warnings is not the only way that we can improve a11y in our applications. We can also inform users of navigation events by updating the title of each page. By announcing route changes in the following way, we have the benefit of alerting users of screen readers while maintaining client-side navigation.

Announcing routes

Another strategy for ensuring a11y of our applications includes announcing our routes. This effectively means that all of our pages include a title so that screen readers can announce the new page to their users. With typical SSR applications, navigation consists of each new page being loaded when navigated to. With SvelteKit, navigation is handled by the client and so full-page reloads are not always necessary. This presents a dilemma for screen readers as they rely on a new title element to be present with each link clicked so that the page may be announced to users.

To play better with screen readers, we can insert a title into each new page we create using the `<svelte:head>` directive:

src/routes/+page.svelte

```
<script>
  import db from 'db';
  import url from 'img/demo.svg';
  let status = db.connection;
  let name = 'World';
</script>
<svelte:head>
  <title>Home</title>
</svelte:head>
<form>
  <label for="name" >What is your name?</label>
  <input type="text" class='name' bind:value={name} />
</form>
<h1>Hello, {name}!</h1>
<p>{status}</p>
<img src={url} alt='demo'>
```

On our application landing page, we've re-added the `alt` attribute to our `<img>` tag, but more importantly, we've set the page title to **Home** by including it in the `<svelte:head>` tag. Let's make a similar change in another file so we can observe how this affects the browsing experience:

src/routes/(site)/about/+page.svelte

```
<svelte:head>
  <title>About</title>
</svelte:head>
<div class='wrapper'>
  <h1>About</h1>
  <p>
    Lorem ipsum dolor ...
  </p>
</div>
```

In our application's **About** page, we've set the title by adding a `<title>` element with the appropriate text and surrounding it with `<svelte:head>` tags. These tags place the content within the document head. To see how this can affect the browsing experience, open the development version of the application and take note of the page title shown in your browser on the home page. Then, click **About** and observe how the title shown in the browser tab changes.

For screen reader applications, this small change allows them to alert users that they have navigated to a new route. Even for users who are not utilizing a screen reader, this is a noticeable improvement over the previous text showing only the site name. If a user were to bookmark a page on this site, the default text would now more accurately reflect the page in question. Not only is this helpful addition for all human users but it can also be a big boost to our application's SEO, as many search engines will take into account page titles when indexing posts.

By announcing routes, we can greatly improve the experience of our application for its users. Next, let's take a look at some other small adjustments that can make big improvements.

Accessibility enhancements

Not all developers nor all of those who utilize screen readers speak English as their primary language. As such, we should be able to adjust our application accordingly. Doing so is fairly straightforward and we can vastly improve the experience for users of assistive technology around the world by making a small note about the language our content is served in. By default, SvelteKit sets the language to English but we can quickly adjust it by changing the `lang` attribute on the `<html>` element in `src/app.html`:

src/app.html

```
<!DOCTYPE html>
<html lang="en">
```

```
    <head>
        <meta charset="utf-8" />
        <link rel="icon" href="%sveltekit.assets%/favicon.png" />
        <meta name="viewport" content="width=device-width" />
        %sveltekit.head%
    </head>
    <body data-sveltekit-preload-data="hover">
        <div style="display: contents">%sveltekit.body%</div>
    </body>
</html>
```

Note the `<html>` element at the top of the file with the `lang` attribute set. Setting the `lang` attribute to the appropriate language, such as `fr` for French or `ar` for Arabic, ensures that screen readers can correctly pronounce or translate the content.

One final a11y improvement we can make in our applications is allowing SvelteKit to manipulate the focus on HTML elements. Normally, when an application is rendered on the server, each new navigation event resets the focus. But in client-side rendered applications, the browser may not detect that a navigation event has occurred and therefore, focus will persist on whatever the currently focused element happens to be. To manage this with a11y in mind, SvelteKit resets focus to the `<body>` element – that is, unless an element has the `autofocus` attribute set, at which point that element will be given focus. Letting SvelteKit's behavior take control of focus comes with the benefit of letting users of screen readers know that a navigation event has occurred.

When it comes to making our applications more accessible to a wider audience, it doesn't take much effort on our part. Doing so improves the user experience, and all of the aforementioned improvements can also boost SEO rankings.

SEO Tips

Aside from making some small a11y improvements in our application, we can keep some other suggestions in mind. Firstly, we should make use of SvelteKit's **Server-Side Rendering** (**SSR**) whenever possible. Doing so ensures the quick delivery of the application as well as makes content easier for search engines to parse. Of course, many search engines now have the capabilities to index client-side rendered content, but the speed and reliability of SSR cannot be discounted. We should only disable SSR if we have a valid reason to.

Another useful tip to consider is the performance of our application. For the most part, we can rely on Vite to tree-shake unused code out of our builds. Smaller bundle sizes mean fewer lines of code to deliver to the client and many search engines rank results based on asset delivery times. See the *Resources* section at the end of this chapter for tools that can deliver insights into your page speeds.

The final useful tip for improving SEO is to leave trailing slashes off route names. Having extra slashes can negatively impact page ranks, so unless you have a valid reason to, consider leaving the page option `trailingSlash` property alone. By following these few tips, we can be sure our SvelteKit application will rank highly in search engine results.

Summary

When it comes to building a successful web application, we must strive to make it accessible to all. The reasons for doing so may be purely selfish by attempting to capture as much of the market as possible, or egalitarian by trying to include users from all walks of the web. It could be that you simply want to be highly ranked in search engine results. Whatever the reasons may be, it's a fairly straightforward process with SvelteKit. We've seen the warnings provided at compile time and we've learned about the benefits of both SEO and a11y when it comes to creating unique page titles. With a few SEO tips to keep in mind, it's easy for our accessible apps to become known to the world.

Having wrapped up this chapter, we've covered nearly everything there is to discuss about SvelteKit. However, technology moves quickly so we can never truly be finished learning. By the time this book is published, there will likely have been more improvements and changes introduced into SvelteKit. To ensure you have the latest information, the next chapter will provide more resources, communities, and examples that are well worth your time to explore.

Resources

- *The A11y Project* – `https://www.a11yproject.com/`
- *MDN Web Docs: Accessibility* – `https://developer.mozilla.org/en-US/docs/Web/Accessibility`
- *Svelte Accessibility Warnings* – `https://svelte.dev/docs#accessibility-warnings`
- *PageSpeed Insights* – `https://pagespeed.web.dev/`

Appendix
Examples and Support

Because learning is a never-ending process and technology moves quickly, this final chapter aims to provide you with the resources you'll need to continue your journey with SvelteKit. In the world of web development, it's rare to see a project that doesn't integrate multiple tools and technologies, so we'll address how we can easily integrate SvelteKit with other frontend tooling. We'll also see some official and community-based resources that are invaluable when it comes to troubleshooting, advancing our knowledge, or discovering new components. After that, we'll wrap things up with a thank-you from the author. Let's finish this book with the following sections:

- Integrations
- More Reading and Resources
- Wrapping up

Afterward, you'll have all the tools and knowledge necessary to go forth and build cool SvelteKit projects.

Technical requirements

The complete code for this chapter is available on GitHub at: `https://github.com/PacktPublishing/SvelteKit-Up-and-Running/tree/tailwind`.

Integrations

When it comes to building modern web applications, it's not uncommon to use a plethora of technologies. Each tool has its place, and it may be the case that a developer is more comfortable with a particular frontend framework than they are with standard CSS. This is fine, as it can speed up development so long as the tools integrate nicely with others. Fortunately for us, SvelteKit works quite well with others.

At the time of writing, Tailwind CSS has become incredibly popular. Tailwind CSS aims to reduce the amount of shipped CSS by only extracting that which is used. This is great to reduce the amount of assets delivered to clients and speed up load times. To showcase how simple it is to integrate a tool such as Tailwind CSS in our existing SvelteKit project, let's work through it. These steps can also be found in the official Tailwind CSS documentation. It's recommended to create a new branch in your repository before starting this process, as it will break some of our existing styles. If you're following along with this book's repository, these examples are available on the `tailwind` branch. To begin, we can install Tailwind along with a couple of other dependencies using the following commands:

```
npm install -D tailwindcss postcss autoprefixer
```

Of course, `tailwindcss` will include the necessary tooling to use Tailwind CSS within our project. The `postcss` dependency will allow us to manipulate CSS files, and `autoprefixer` is a `postcss` plugin that will automatically inject the appropriate vendor prefixes into our generated CSS. Once we have added the dependencies to our development environment, we can use the following command to initialize our Tailwind project. It will create the necessary `tailwind.config.js` and `postcss.config.js` files:

```
npx tailwindcss init -p
```

After initializing `tailwindcss`, we can open `svelte.config.js` and import the `vitePreprocess` module. This will enable us to process `<style>` tags throughout our Svelte components:

svelte.config.js

```
import adapter from '@sveltejs/adapter-auto';
import { vitePreprocess } from '@sveltejs/kit/vite';
const config = {
    kit: {
        adapter: adapter(),
        alias: {
            db: '/src/db.js',
            img: '/src/lib/images'
        }
    },
    preprocess: vitePreprocess()
};
export default config;
```

Now that we have imported `vitePreprocess`, we can ensure that Tailwind CSS knows about the paths to our components. We can do this by updating `tailwind.config.js`, like so:

tailwind.config.js

```js
/** @type {import('tailwindcss').Config} */
export default {
  content: ['./src/**/*.{html,js,svelte,ts}'],
  theme: {
    extend: {},
  },
  plugins: [],
}
```

Noticeably, we only need to change the paths available in the `content` array property to point to our `src/` directory and ensure that the `.svelte` file type is recognized, along with other standard file types.

We can then create a singular `app.css` file, where we can import all of Tailwind's functionality using the `@tailwind` directive:

src/app.css

```css
@tailwind base;
@tailwind components;
@tailwind utilities;
```

If you've been paying attention, the next step should be straightforward. We then import `src/app.css` into our root layout component:

src/routes/+layout.svelte

```svelte
<script>
  import '/src/reset.css';
  import '/src/app.css';
  import Nav from '$lib/Nav.svelte';
  import Notify from '$lib/Notify.svelte';
  export let data;
</script>
<div class='wrapper'>
  <div class='nav'>
    <div class='menu'>
      <Nav />
    </div>
```

```
      <div class='notifications'>
        <Notify count={data.notifications.count}/>
      </div>
    </div>
    <div class='content bg-orange-300'>
      <slot />
    </div>
    <div class='footer'>
      This is my footer
    </div>
  </div>
  <!-- <style> omitted for brevity -->
```

Of course, we've already imported `reset.css`, so there will be conflicts with the existing CSS throughout our project. Ensure your development environment is running with `npm run dev`. To prevent completely breaking our project, we've only set the background on the `.content` element to a light orange color provided by Tailwind CSS, but we'll definitely notice other changes applied throughout the project. Now would be an excellent time to explore the practice of utility-first CSS if you have not yet done so.

We saw the manual way of integrating another tool such as Tailwind CSS, but we're talking about SvelteKit, where things just work. If these steps are too much to remember, there is a simpler way. Try creating yet another branch based off of `main` in your project repository and use the following command to do essentially the same thing we just did. Again, if you're following along with the book repository, this code can be found in the `tailwind-add` branch:

```
npx svelte-add@latest tailwindcss
```

We can follow along with the prompts, and once we've installed the dependencies with `npm install`, our project will have Tailwind CSS integrated! By using the community-maintained `svelte-add` project, we can quickly and easily import templates that integrate various technologies with our SvelteKit project. For instance, if you prefer to use SCSS/Sass flavors when writing CSS, you can use the `scss` custom adder, like so:

```
npx svelte-add@latest scss
```

As we can see, it's not difficult to incorporate different technologies with SvelteKit. While we can incorporate these other toolchains manually, it's also easily done with community-provided resources. Let's take a look at more community resources to see what else is out there!

More Reading and Resources

As previously demonstrated, the community resources surrounding SvelteKit can be excellent to save us time and mental overhead, allowing us to focus on building our applications. This book would not have been possible without the community around SvelteKit. If you're looking to expand on your SvelteKit knowledge, assist others, or create your own SvelteKit extensions, consider the various resources listed next!

SvelteKit Documentation

The documentation provided on the official SvelteKit website will likely be the best resource you'll find for information about the framework. It's incredibly thorough and constantly updated to reflect changes within the framework. Be sure to start here for any questions you may have about SvelteKit:

```
https://kit.svelte.dev
```

SvelteKit Tutorial

To thoroughly test your SvelteKit knowledge and learn more than this book could cover, check out the official SvelteKit tutorial:

```
https://learn.svelte.dev/tutorial
```

Svelte and SvelteKit chat

Have a question or just want to chat with others that are using SvelteKit? The official Discord server is the place to go:

```
https://svelte.dev/chat
```

Independent Creators

There are too many great writers and creators working with SvelteKit to list here, but a couple of this author's favorites are Rodney Johnson and Josh Collinsworth. Collinsworth provides the excellent SvelteKit static blog starter template we saw in *Chapter 8*, and Johnson creates informative tutorial videos and articles:

- Rodney Johnson: `https://rodneylab.com/`
- Josh Collinsworth: `https://joshcollinsworth.com/`

Svelte Society

When it comes to finding Svelte and SvelteKit community resources, Svelte Society has you covered, whether you're looking for templates, components, adders, or more. They even organize Svelte events, so if you're looking to meet other Svelte developers in your area, you should start here:

`https://sveltesociety.dev/`

SvelteKit Repository

As with many open source projects, the code behind SvelteKit is freely available to view on GitHub. If you believe you've found a bug specific to the framework, consider searching the issues here, and if you don't see your problem listed, contribute by submitting it! SvelteKit developers constantly accept pull requests and appreciate any help they can get:

`https://github.com/sveltejs/kit`

As with many open source projects, the community and documentation can make or break a project. Because of the excellent support behind SvelteKit, it's hard to imagine a future where people don't constantly evangelize about SvelteKit and Svelte.

Wrapping up

If you've made it this far, then thank you for staying with me. I hope the material and knowledge provided here can be of assistance with your SvelteKit projects. If you've enjoyed this book, then do share it with friends, colleagues, and acquaintances who are interested in learning a new JS framework. As this is my first book, it's certainly been a journey for me, and I've learned much about the writing process. If you're interested in finding more technical texts by me, I write at `https://www.closingtags.com` about web development and web-adjacent technologies. If you build something cool with SvelteKit, I'd love to hear about it. I can be reached via the contact form on my website. Thanks again, and I look forward to seeing what you build.

Summary

That's it, you've finished the book! If you still have questions about the various workings of SvelteKit, look into the previously provided community resources. You'll find everything necessary to expand your SvelteKit knowledge and see what others in the community are doing. Because SvelteKit integrates so well with many other tools, it should be a breeze to incorporate it with your existing workflows. I look forward to seeing what you build with it. Thanks again!

Resources

- Tailwind CSS: `https://tailwindcss.com`
- Svelte Add: `https://github.com/svelte-add/svelte-add`

Index

A

accessibility enhancements 128, 129
actions
  analyzing 60
  database setup 61
  login action 63-65
  passwords 62, 63
  security 62, 63
  working 38-40
adapters 88
  adapter-cloudflare 90-93
  adapter-node 88-90
  adapter-static 93, 94
advanced layouts 79-81
API endpoints 40, 41
app
  adapting 88
assets
  importing 112-114

B

bcrypt 62
Bootstrap 112

C

Cascading Style Sheet (CSS) 112
Chrome
  cookie, creating for 55
client
  data loading 46, 47
client-side rendering (CSR) 38
Compile-Time Checks 126, 127
Content Delivery Network (CDN) 15, 115
Content Security Policy (CSP) 14
cookie
  creating, for Chrome 55
  creating, for Firefox 55
cross-site request forgery
  (CSRF) attacks 15, 89
cross-site scripting (XSS) attacks 14
Crypto Web API 61
Custom CSS Reset 112

D

dynamic pages
  creating 32-36

E

encoding 78, 79
enhance 66
error handling 106-108

F

fetch API 20-22
file paths 116
Firefox
    cookie, creating for 55
form
    enhancing 66
    setting up 58-60
FormData API 23, 24, 62, 65

H

Hello World application 8
hooks 97
    server hooks 98-104
    shared hooks 104-106
    using 98
Hot Module Replacement (HMR) 8

I

images
    versus styles 115
imports
    customizing 115
independent creators 135
Integrated Development
    Environment (IDE) 4
integrations 131-134

L

layouts
    creating 42-44
    data loading 47-52
Long-Term Support (LTS) 4

M

matcher
    applying 77
matching 77
module analysis
    $app/environment module 120
    $app/forms module 120
    $app/navigation module 120, 121
    $app/paths module 121
    $app/stores module 121
    $service-worker module 122
modules, for secret keeping
    $env/dynamic/private 123
    $env/dynamic/public 123
    $env/static/private 122
    $env/static/public 123

N

Node Version Manager (NVM) 4
notification badge 49

O

optional parameters
    using 72-74

P

Page Options 87

page options, server pages 37

  client-side rendering (CSR) 38

  prerender 38

  server-side rendering (SSR) 38

personal access token 98

picomatch pattern 116

production build, of application

  creating 86, 87

  creating, consideration 87

Progressive Web App (PWA) 46

project structure, SvelteKit 6

  app.html 7

  src/ 7

  src/lib/ 7

  src/routes/ 7

  static/ 6

  tests/ 6

R

regular expressions (regex) 77

RequestEvent

  destructuring 52-55, 101

rest parameters 74-76

routes

  announcing 127, 128

S

Search Engine Optimization (SEO) 125

  tips 129

secrets

  keeping 122

server hooks 98-103

server pages

  actions 38-40

  creating 37

  load() 37

  page options 37

server-side rendering (SSR) 38, 129

shared hooks 104-106

single-page application (SPA) 38

snapshots 66-68

sorting 78

styles

  versus images 115

svelte.config.js file 12

SvelteKit

  installing 5, 6

  project structure 6

  resources 135

SvelteKit chat

  reference link 135

SvelteKit configuration 12

  alias 13, 14

  appDir 14

  csp 14

  csrf 15

  env 15

  prerender 16

SvelteKit configuration options

  files.assets 116

  paths.assets 116

  paths.base 116

  paths.relative 116

SvelteKit documentation 135

  reference link 135

SvelteKit Repository 136

  reference link 136

SvelteKit tutorial 135

  reference link 135

Svelte Society 136
    URL 136

T

Tailwind CSS 112
TypeScript (TS) 5

U

Unicode 79
universal load timing 47
Universally Unique Identifier (UUID) 61
URL API 25, 26

V

Visual Studio Code (VS Code) 4
Vite configuration 16
    assetsInclude 116
    build 17
    optimizeDeps 18
    plugins 17
    preview 18
    server 17
    ssr 18

W

Web APIs
    fetch 20, 21
    fetch API 22
    FormData API 23, 24
    URL API 25, 26

Z

zero-config adapter 12

Packtpub.com

Subscribe to our online digital library for full access to over 7,000 books and videos, as well as industry leading tools to help you plan your personal development and advance your career. For more information, please visit our website.

Why subscribe?

- Spend less time learning and more time coding with practical eBooks and Videos from over 4,000 industry professionals

- Improve your learning with Skill Plans built especially for you

- Get a free eBook or video every month

- Fully searchable for easy access to vital information

- Copy and paste, print, and bookmark content

Did you know that Packt offers eBook versions of every book published, with PDF and ePub files available? You can upgrade to the eBook version at packtpub.com and as a print book customer, you are entitled to a discount on the eBook copy. Get in touch with us at customercare@packtpub.com for more details.

At www.packtpub.com, you can also read a collection of free technical articles, sign up for a range of free newsletters, and receive exclusive discounts and offers on Packt books and eBooks.

Other Books You May Enjoy

If you enjoyed this book, you may be interested in these other books by Packt:

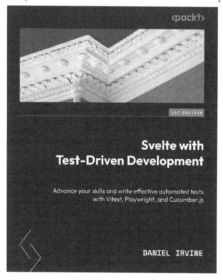

Svelte with Test-Driven Development

Daniel Irvine

ISBN: 978-1-83763-833-8

- Create clear and concise Vitest unit tests helping the implementation of Svelte components.

- Use Playwright and Cucumber.js to develop end-to-end tests that simulate user interactions and test the functionality of your application.

- Leverage component mocks to isolate and test individual components.

- Write unit tests for a range of Svelte framework features.

- Explore effective refactoring techniques to keep your Svelte application code and test suites clean.

Full Stack Web Development with Remix

Andre Landgraf

ISBN: 978-1-80107-529-9

- Understand Remix's philosophy and guiding principles.
- Increase your expertise in the web platform which you can take anywhere.
- Master data mutations, routing, error handling, and state management with Remix
- Learn how to build with accessibility and progressive enhancement in mind.
- Familiarize yourself with advanced topics such as caching strategies, real-time communication, and developing for the edge.
- Work with state-of-the-art technologies such as the edge, multi-regional databases, and Redis.

Packt is searching for authors like you

If you're interested in becoming an author for Packt, please visit `authors.packtpub.com` and apply today. We have worked with thousands of developers and tech professionals, just like you, to help them share their insight with the global tech community. You can make a general application, apply for a specific hot topic that we are recruiting an author for, or submit your own idea.

Share Your Thoughts

Now you've finished *SvelteKit Up and Running*, we'd love to hear your thoughts! Scan the QR code below to go straight to the Amazon review page for this book and share your feedback or leave a review on the site that you purchased it from.

`https://packt.link/r/1-804-61548-X`

Your review is important to us and the tech community and will help us make sure we're delivering excellent quality content.

Download a free PDF copy of this book

Thanks for purchasing this book!

Do you like to read on the go but are unable to carry your print books everywhere?

Is your eBook purchase not compatible with the device of your choice?

Don't worry, now with every Packt book you get a DRM-free PDF version of that book at no cost.

Read anywhere, any place, on any device. Search, copy, and paste code from your favorite technical books directly into your application.

The perks don't stop there, you can get exclusive access to discounts, newsletters, and great free content in your inbox daily

Follow these simple steps to get the benefits:

1. Scan the QR code or visit the link below

https://packt.link/free-ebook/9781804615485

2. Submit your proof of purchase
3. That's it! We'll send your free PDF and other benefits to your email directly

Printed by Amazon Italia Logistica S.r.l.
Torrazza Piemonte (TO), Italy

49903986R00094